Aiming high

Approaches to teaching 'A' level

CiLT
Centre for Information
on Language Teaching and Research

The Centre for Information on Language Teaching and Research provides a complete range of services for language professionals in every stage and sector of education, and in business, in support of its brief to promote Britain's foreign language capability.

CILT is a registered charity, supported by Central Government grants. CILT is based in Covent Garden, London, and its services are delivered through a national collaborative network of regional Comenius Centres in England, the National Comenius Centre of Wales, Scottish CILT and Northern Ireland CILT.

Aiming high

Approaches to teaching 'A' level

Edited by
Glenis Shaw

with contributions from

Glenis Shaw and Agnès Anciaux, Tony Lonsdale,
Betty Hunt, Lid King, Jim Anderson, Salvador Estébanez,
Susan Tebbutt, Hilary Macdougall and Gareth Thomas

CiLT
Centre for Information
on Language Teaching and Research

The views expressed in this publication are the contributors' and do not necessarily represent those of CILT.

First published in 1996

Reprinted 1997

Copyright © 1996 Centre for Information on Language Teaching and Research

ISBN 1 874016 74 7

A catalogue record for this book is available from the British Library
Cover by Marc Padellec
Printed in Great Britain by Redwood Books, Trowbridge

Published by the Centre for Information on Language Teaching and Research, 20 Bedfordbury, Covent Garden, London WC2N 4LB

CILT Publications are available from: Grantham Book Services, Isaac Newton Way, Alma Park Industrial Estate, Grantham, Lincs NG31 8SD. Tel: 01476 567 421. Fax: 01476 590 223. Book trade representation (UK and Ireland): Broadcast Book Services, 24 De Montfort Road, London SW16 1LZ. Tel: 0181 677 5129.

Contents

The contributors

Agnès Anciaux
Head of Modern Languages, Langley Park Girls School, Beckenham

Jim Anderson
Head of Languages, John Roan School, Greenwich

Salvador Estébanez
Spanish Embassy Education Office

Betty Hunt
Author, formerly Westminster College, Oxford

Lid King
Director, CILT

Tony Lonsdale
Deputy Head, Cardinal Newman College, Preston

Hilary MacDougall
Head of Modern Languages, St Paul's Girls School

Glenis Shaw
Language Teaching Adviser, CILT

Susan Tebbut
Sheffield Hallam University, formerly Head of Languages, King Edward School, Sheffield

Gareth Thomas
Pro Vice Chancellor, Coventry University

Preface

The introduction of new syllabuses for 'A' level and 'AS' level examinations from September 1995, based on the revised subject core from SCAA, provided the impetus for many modern languages teachers to re-evaluate and revise their teaching.

The new syllabuses are designed to achieve a natural progression from GCSE. They contain three elements: knowledge and understanding, concepts and skills, and assessment objectives. Permeating all three parts of the core are the complementary elements of knowledge of contemporary society and linguistic competence. Other aspects of the examinations themselves also have significant implications for teachers: almost all questions are to be answered in the target language; there is greater emphasis on the transfer of meaning and the integration of the four skills; there is a choice of assessment mode — coursework, modular or terminal.

Aiming high brings together contributions from speakers at a CILT conference on the teaching of languages to 'A' and 'AS' levels. The conference addressed issues around one central theme — how can we help all our students to achieve their full potential? This book, therefore, offers reflections and tried and tested ideas from colleagues who are working with 'A' level and 'AS' level students. They have provided us with a bank of examples and suggestions which can be adapted to suit the needs of both teacher and learner.

Introduction

The 'A' level examination — a decade of change

Glenis Shaw

Until 1988 the vast majority of students taking Language 'A' levels followed a well-worn route which had existed apparently since time immemorial. The final examination consisted of translation from and into the target language, the writing of general essays (in the target language) and literary essays usually on four texts (in English). Students would have some practice in dictation and a fairly perfunctory experience of 'oral discussion'. The teaching may well have been a fairly genteel and relaxed affair, reflecting these assessment priorities.

By 1990 the situation had changed out of all recognition. Translation into the language being studied had disappeared completely from some boards' syllabuses, and in others it had become a short response to a stimulus. The study of literature was in most cases optional, and in all cases less important. Listening and speaking tests accounted for up to fifty per cent of the final assessment. Although the speed of change caused concern for some people it is worth remembering the reasons for it, particularly as these have an effect on later developments. Perhaps the most fundamental one was also the most simple: **during the 1980s traditional language 'A' levels were failing the majority of pupils** and numbers taking them were declining.

New courses for a new kind of student

It might well be supposed that the main reason for this decline was not a sudden change in the linguistic capabilities of post-16 pupils but the unsuitability of the examinations for the majority of students. For although there were fewer people taking 'A' level, overall more pupils were studying languages in schools. They were, however, following courses based on more communicative principles and with more practical outcomes than the traditional 'A' level. The first GCSEs were taken in 1988 and new skill-based and practical courses (RSA, Institute of Linguists, FLAW, etc) were being introduced. The Technical and Vocational Education Initiative (TVEI) also had an influence on language courses.

It was certainly the view of the examination boards that something had to be done to make 'A' level more relevant to students. From the early eighties a number of working groups were set up to devise new syllabuses. Their starting point was often the report of 'Working Party no 28' — *New patterns in sixth form modern language studies*,[1] which envisaged a more skill-based syllabus, involving the teaching of language through culture and the development of study skills and independent learning.

Similar ideas were further developed in *French 16–19: a new perspective*,[2] published in 1981, which not only described the possible aims and target groups of the 'new 'A' level' but outlined many of the methodological approaches which have been so influential in the 80s and 90s. The writers of *French 16–19* foresaw that the majority of post-16 students would be non-specialists seeking to extend their language competence while developing other skills and areas of knowledge. They also saw that the main purpose of the 'A' level course should be for **use** rather than **analysis** of the language. The 'A' level course *must have as its central purpose the development of practical language skills.*

In this respect the new 'A' level was seen very much as the continuation of GCSE. The syllabuses all claimed such compatibility and despite the differences between them — they all shared the basic communicative philosophy of *French 16–19*.

In theory then, teaching a post-16 course should have been more straightforward than it had been in the past. There was at least a perception of continuity with what had gone before (GCSE) and, whatever the differences between courses and syllabuses, there were certain shared assumptions:

- a wider, less specialised target group;
- language learning based on authentic — often contemporary — texts;
- a new importance given to the development of communicative skills;
- resource-based teaching organised around topics.

Organising an integrated programme

There was little doubt that the new 'A' level demanded more of the teacher and these demands began in the sphere of planning and organisation. According to some experienced teachers on a CILT in-service course the new GCSE examination meant that the incoming Year 12 language student could often *speak with confidence, read for detailed meaning and recall defined vocabulary* but found it difficult to generate new language, read extensively for gist and interpret unfamiliar text. If these interpretations were correct then there were a number of implications for the teaching programme in the first year of the 'A' level course in terms of extending the competence and language experience of the students.

The next logical step in the establishment of a teaching programme involved decisions about **Topics** (the content of the course), **Language** (appropriate syntax, lexis for various stages of the course) and **Skills** (the competences needed in order to access this content and language). It was here that the change in approach from the earlier period was most marked. One of the most rewarding and exciting things about the new courses was the possibility of introducing students to a whole range of text types (novels, magazines, TV, radio) and of subject matter to **involve** them and **excite** their interest. It was also an area which demanded a great deal of the 'A' level teacher — not so much in finding materials but in selecting and using them, in ensuring that the ensuing programme was both **integrated** and **coherent**.

Collaboration with colleagues became of the utmost importance. For as well as realistic preparation, the teacher of 'A' level needed to develop a degree of cooperation which was rare before the introduction of the new courses, especially where classes were shared. It was certainly desirable to work collaboratively on the choice and resourcing of topics and on the production of materials.

Attention also had to be given to the **involvement of the students** in these processes. One of the difficulties for them was that in trying to adapt to advanced language work the programme could appear incoherent — reading an article one day, then watching some TV, discussion, grammar . . . Experience suggested that students became better learners if the teaching processes were made explicit, for example, by the distribution of a half termly programme of objectives, including materials and tasks. The existence of such a programme is invaluable not only as a support to the student but as a check on the teaching and learning process.

Resource-based learning

It is never easy to summarise a process as complex as teaching and learning. But if there were two basic assumptions underlying the 'new' approaches to language learning at advanced level they were:

- that the core of language learning was the development of communicative competence;
- that the starting point for language acquisition was not grammar (rules) but 'authentic text' (raw material).

By text was meant written, spoken or visual materials.

The role of the teacher then became one of enabling students to 'access' text, to derive meaning from it, to acquire, practise — and ultimately reuse as his or her own — the language contained within it. The teacher was not so much a purveyor of knowledge as (in the jargon of the eighties) a facilitator. As a corollary of this the student took a more active role in the learning process, and by implication became a much more efficient and capable learner.

The key point of these communicative approaches is not so much that the material being used is authentic — since at 'A' level that had often if not always been the case — but rather that the text is being used to help the learner acquire language, and that the learner does this by working on (interacting with) the text. The teacher helps the learner approach the text by making it more accessible. At the same time there needs to be some level of difficulty (effort, challenge) if the learner is to actually acquire language.

More recently this aspect of learner involvement or interaction has been given greater attention than had previously been the case. On one level this has meant giving more attention to the way people learn — what are commonly called 'study skills'. It has been seen as important to include in the teaching programme such tasks as 'use of the dictionary', 'learning how to read, listen', etc. These skills are not innate. They have to be learned.

A further development of this learner involvement has been the understanding that, despite what has been said above, language acquisition is not simply **from** the text. It is the result of interaction between the learner and text. The learner, especially the advanced learner, brings a considerable amount of prior knowledge, both about the world (conceptual) and about language (linguistic) to his or her confrontation with the text. It would therefore appear sensible consciously to use that existing knowledge in order to speed up the process of acquisition.

What about grammar?

One issue which continues to tax teachers at this level in particular is the question of grammar. What should be introduced? When and how? Unfortunately there does not appear to be a simple answer and indeed what works for one student is a total failure with another.

Traditionally grammar was taught by rule and supported by example. This approach still continues, often in the form of 'intensive grammar grind' at the beginning of the 'A' level course. There is no evidence that it is particularly successful. On the other hand there are undoubtedly occasions when with certain learners this may work.

The new approaches have suggested an alternative model — acquiring grammar through study of text. Although this seems a sounder approach it may have contributed to a certain lack of structure to some pupils' grammatical understanding. It all depends on what grammatical points they have studied.

It seems clear enough that the advanced learner needs a grammar — a basic understanding of structures which will enable him or her to generate language. The new language learner is also unlikely to benefit from a traditional rule-based approach but will often end up confused in the absence of rules. It seems that teachers are feeling their way towards a hybrid approach based on 'grammar in use'. This implies the development of at least an outline of an idea of grammatical progression and the selection of texts to support that outline. It also implies giving students time to ask about what they do not understand (the tutorial).

Where next?

In the next couple of years pupils will be emerging from the National Curriculum and the new GCSEs with slightly different skills than previously. They will (hopefully) be more used to hearing and using the target language, have already learnt dictionary skills and they should be more at ease with modern technology such as CD-ROM and Satellite TV.

The new 'A' level examinations are seen as a continuum from GCSE, requiring an increased use of target language and a deeper knowledge of the National Curriculum Areas of Experience. Both literary and non literary topics must be taught and questions answered in the target language. This has further implications for planning both of topics and also of progression in learning the language. A requirement for knowledge of the culture and contemporary society of a country where the target language is spoken has implications for resources which will need to be kept up to date. A greater emphasis on the transfer of meaning requires a greater emphasis on accuracy. The integration of the four skills has changed the format of examinations but probably does not effect classroom teaching so much where skills were already often integrated. Teachers of 'A' level courses are having to choose their syllabus with care, deciding between modular, coursework and 100 per cent examinations for their students. All syllabuses, however, must contain the revised subject core set out by SCAA, containing three elements: knowledge and understanding, concepts and skills and assessment objectives.

As we head towards the millennium we see an increasing number of students studying a foreign language, although dual and even triple linguists are becoming rarer (though not extinct). Vocational courses and the Dearing review of post-16 education will also affect the opportunities on offer for students of advanced languages. There is a desire to see the 'Gold Standard' maintained in both traditional and 'applied' 'A' levels. There are already Business 'A' levels to consider. Students will study languages in ever greater variety of combinations so that 'A' level will become more practical in orientation while allowing more space for individual interests. As we move into the new 'A' levels if we can be certain of anything it is that change will continue.

References

1   Schools Council for Curriculum and Examinations, *New patterns in sixth form modern languages studies*, Working Paper no 28 (Evans/Methuen Educational, 1970)

2   Report of the French 16–19 Study Group, *French 16–19: a new perspective* (Hodder and Stoughton, 1981)

'A'

Part one

•

First year

Chapter 1

Bridging the gap between GCSE and 'A' level

Glenis Shaw and Agnès Anciaux

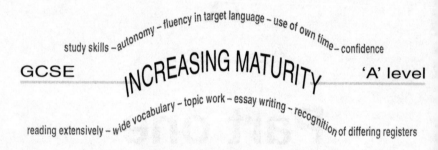

study skills – autonomy – fluency in target language – use of own time – confidence

GCSE INCREASING MATURITY 'A' level

reading extensively – wide vocabulary – topic work – essay writing – recognition of differing registers

The whole 'A' level course is in itself a bridge between the GCSE and the 'A' level examinations. The first step out onto this bridge can be the most difficult, and where the gap can be the biggest. Year 11 learners leave school in June as pupils and come back in September as students. They feel different. The situation is different.

They may have changed institutions, they may be taught in a sixth form block, there will be a new social context and they may not know the teachers. They may well be feeling anxious, and that others have done better in the GCSE examinations.

The teacher needs to create, as quickly as possible, a group that can work together positively, a group where individuals can collaborate, or work independently, feel confident and that they are progressing. Students need to find their new 'A' level course interesting, even exciting. It needs to be different and that little bit more difficult — challenging enough to need to work and try hard but not too difficult to feel they cannot cope.

What do students bring to the 'A' level course?

- A feeling of success from their GCSE examination results.
- Motivation and enthusiam: they have chosen to do the modern language.
- Hopefulness; they are ready to work, full of good intentions and goodwill.

What skills and knowledge do they bring?

- Willingness to communicate orally.
- A readiness to tackle unfamiliar texts and make guesses, in reading and listening.
- A familiarity with certain topics.

What are their main needs?

Their knowledge of grammar is often basic and perfunctory. Grammar grind can be soul destroying, but focusing on such areas as verbs and tenses through interesting and motivating tasks is a necessity.

Students need to begin to read and listen more extensively. Bridging the gap means introducing longer and more varied texts to increase vocabulary and awareness of register.

Certainly they need general study skills. Research has shown, as far as modern languages are concerned, that students are anxious about grammar and its terminology, learning a large amount of vocabulary and writing essays in the target language.

What about the teacher?

There is also a gap in teaching techniques. We have our Key Stage 4 methodology and an 'A' level methodology, but nothing to cover the transitional period.

We need to provide sufficient support for practice and reinforcement activities prior to production. We need to think carefully about our expectations of students at this time. We should be aware of a sudden change of emphasis from communicating the message to a requirement for greater accuracy, especially in written work.

We also need to remember that we are responsible for developing students' interests, thought processes and cognitive faculties. We must move on from buying bread and asking the way to the station! We must provide them with the tools to sustain a logical discussion, explain a point of view — in short, express opinions.

Developing effective learning

The aim of the first few weeks is to prepare students for the main body of the 'A' level course, to help them become effective and independent learners and to provide them with the tools to achieve this. An induction course might contain some of the following:

Study skills

How to organise their work and take notes. Included in this might be ground rules on the use of the target language.

How to learn

Different ways of coping with new vocabulary learning; choosing some words/lexical items for themselves; realising that at some point grammar too has to be learnt, e.g. strong verbs.

Grammar terminology

Needed for short cuts in understanding and learning; needed in order to understand language in greater detail and how it works, even for using the dictionary — although as the National Curriculum works through we should be able to expect some consistent prior knowledge about grammar and dictionaries.

adjective	**nominativo, va** *adj* GRAM nominative ‖ COM nominal (título) ‖ bearing a person's name (cheque).
	◆ *m* GRAM nominative; *nominativo absoluto* nominative absolute.
feminine noun	**nominilla** *f* pay warrant, voucher.
	non *adj* (p us) odd, uneven (impar).
figurative, familiar	◆ *m pl* odds; *jugar a pares y nones* to play odds and evens ‖ — FIG & FAM *decir nones* to refuse point blank ‖ *quedar de non* to be odd man out, to be left out, to be left without a partner.
plural	**nona** *f* nones *pl* (hora canónica) ‖ nones *pl* (del calendario romano).
	nonio *m* TECN nonius, vernier.
	nono, na *adj* ninth ‖ *décimo nono* nineteenth.
latin phrase	**non plus ultra** *loc lat* nec plus ultra.
	nopal *m* BOT nopal, prickly pear.
	normando, da *adj/s* Norman.
	◆ *m* Norman French (lengua) ‖ HIST Norseman (vikingo).
	normativo, va *adj* normative.
adjective/ masculine noun	**nornordeste** *adj/sm* north-northeast.
	nornoroeste; nornorueste *adj/adv/sm* north-northwest.
adverb	

How to structure an essay

The 'A' level essay is essentially different from any writing at GCSE level. The first essay should be collaborative and guided, in order to make clear the structure, i.e. introduction, discussion and conclusion. Mind mapping can be done as a joint activity in class or groups or as an individual brainstorming activity. It is a more disciplined approach than brainstorming, which leads to the developing of ideas or themes for an essay in a structured and balanced way.

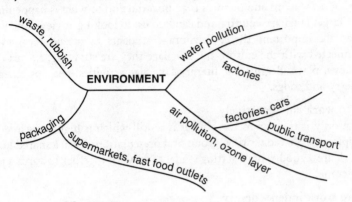

How to cope with texts

'A' level requires a variety of different texts and registers. Begin small, but show the need to look for key words and phrases. Teach how to summarise, categorise, analyse and report. Start to use the technique of talking about the text, around the text and away from the text.

Study skills and language learning activities

Degree of support/ independence	Intellectual processes	Performance tasks

I Working within the text
Discovering the text
Collecting language/
ideas
	• decoding
	• recognising
	• identifying
	• selecting (analytical
	• classifying processes)
	• sequencing
		• transcribing
		• completing
		• note-taking
		• making lists of
		  language and facts
		• asking/answering
		  questions

II Working around the text *Sorting, practising* *language/ideas*	• matching • re-organising • inferring • interpreting • selecting/rejecting • evaluating	• summarising • renarrating • expanding condensed material • elucidating • interpreting
III Working away from the text *Independent,* *integrated use of newly* *and previously* *acquired language/* *ideas/knowledge*		• role playing • dramatising • adapting • counter-argument • personal/imaginative writing
At all stages: cross-reference to other sources and materials, including reference books, teacher, tape, video, film, native speakers, dictionary		

from *German for 'A' level: a resource-based approach* (CILT, 1985)

Developing a growing awareness of the social, political and cultural aspects of the language and country

Using news items and pictures is an introduction to what is happening in the target language country and can lead on to looking at views and issues that are important there. Encourage students to attend local events connected with the culture and language they are studying, e.g. art exhibitions, plays. Begin some literary language activities, perhaps based on poetry and songs.

How to work collaboratively

Not only is this supportive, but it is a skill which is highly regarded by employers. Shared writing, group oral presentations, even a shared homework are a good way of getting students to work together towards a joint outcome.

How to work independently

Give them the skills, by careful explanation of the steps to be taken and resources to be found, to be able to work independently on listening and reading texts at home, to self-access electronic resources and to interrogate reference materials. This could lead to taped oral presentations or preparation of a timed individual presentation on a particular topic where the rest of the group can then ask questions.

Assessment

This must be clear. Do you mark it at GCSE, intermediate or 'A' level standard at the beginning of the course? Whatever you choose, your criteria must be clear to students and must show a regard for their personal achievement and progression. A good starting point is to take three or four language structures that the group as a whole has found difficulty with and concentrate on these in detail.

Coping with homework

Many students have Saturday jobs and less time for the six hours of 'A' level home study that has been a normal requirement in the past. Students need advice on time management, using reference materials and guidelines on the required outcome of the homework, e.g. 'Write an essay on . . .' needs a specific outline, length and criteria for success at this stage.

Some ideas for the first weeks

Many of these are of course ideal preparations for the GCSE too.

Oral activities

1 Buddy talk — with a partner, have a regular five-minute conversation each lesson on any topic of interest (e.g. *Match of the day*, last night's *Neighbours* episode). The students can choose something that has interested them or the teacher may choose a particular topic in the news.

2 Invitations — have a list of invitations to go out in the evening, acceptances and refusals. In threes, one invites, one accepts, one declines.

Einladungen

Möchtest du ins Kino gehen?
Möchtest du in die Disco gehen?
Willst du ins Café gehen?
Wollen wir in die Kneipe gehen?
Möchtest du zum Fußball?
Wollen wir Tennis spielen?
Wollen wir schwimmen gehen?
Willst du an mir vorbeikommen?

Willst du in die Stadt gehen?
Wollen wir uns ein Video holen?
Möchtest du einen Ausflug nach Potsdam machen?
Wollen wir Eis essen gehen?
Hast du Lust spazieren zu gehen?
Wie wäre es mit einem Bier?
Kommst du mit kegeln?

Ausreden Ja danke

Bitte! Wie herrlich!
Prima!
Das wäre eine schöne Idee.
Wann denn?
Heute nicht, aber morgen habe ich Zeit.
Danke für die Einladung. Ich nehme sie an!
Natürlich. Immer mit dir!
Ich finde das eine tolle Idee.
Ja gerne.
Wenn du darauf bestehst.
Wann, wie, wo und was kostet das?
Wie nett von dir. Aber selbstverständlich.
Lust hab' ich immer!
Gut. Und Geld hab' ich auch.

Ausreden Nein danke

Ich habe keine Lust/keinen Bock.
Ich muß zu Hause helfen, Großreine machen.
Ich muß auf meine kleine Schwester/auf meinen kleinen Bruder aufpassen.
Ich muß das Auto waschen.
Tut mir leid, kein Geld/keine Knete. Ich bin blank.
Ich fühle mich nicht ganz wohl.
Ich habe schon was anderes vor.
Wir kriegen Besuch.
Keine Zeit.
Wir haben den Maler.
Ich habe Kopfschmerzen.
Ich habe einen Kater.

---

3 News reporter — one or two students send news back from Britain to the home country, e.g. the latest about the royal family.

4 Just a minute — talk for a minute on a topic (initially one based on vocabulary learnt at GCSE) taken out of a hat.

5   Picture study — look at a picture for two minutes. Take it away and ask students what they can remember about it.

6   Newspaper photos — make an OHT of an interesting/intriguing picture from that week's newspaper. Ask students to talk about it, i.e. a complete description, and then to discuss around the subject, e.g. a picture of a bomb blast would first elicit a description of the scene followed by a discussion of the cause which might lead on to an expression (very brief at this stage) of an opinion about terrorism in general.

Listening activities

1   Noise levels — a series of sounds on tape (can be bought commercially). Students describe what is happening and invent a story.

2   Soundtrack — in pairs, one student watches a video, one listens. The one who has listened tells the story to the student who has been watching, who then corrects it. *Mr Bean* is excellent for this.

3   Song time — listen to a song. Fill in the gaps in the text, e.g. all verbs or rhyming words. Or cut the lines of the text up and have students put them into order as they listen to the song.

4   Key phrases — choose from written sentences the ones which apply to a piece of listening material. Put them in the order that you hear them in the text.

5   Listen to the news — fill in a grid stating topic, people, places and times.

Reading activities

1   Crazy mail — phrases and sentences in an envelope need to be put in order to make a story.

2   Questionnaires — taken from teenage magazines in the target language.

3   Short story — read a short story and re-tell it from another character's point of view.

4   Diary — read a diary and relate everything you learn about the writer (good for empathy).

5   Travel brochure — read the text and find three key words or phrases from each section to produce a summary of what the town/area/resort has to offer.

Writing activities

1   Storytelling — use a picture story for collaborative writing, with teacher acting as scribe. Add adjectives, adverbs, etc to polish up the story. Write up for homework.

2 Letter writing — take a long letter (perhaps one you have had from a friend) in the target language, with all the verbs missing. Students replace the verbs.

Berlin, den 11.5.95

Liebe Glenis !

Erst wollte ich Dich anrufen, aber dann ist mir eingefallen, daß Du ja auch gerne Post bekommst. Darum möchte ich Dir schreiben, wie gut es mir diesmal in London gefallen hat. Besonders schön war das Wochenende, das ich mit Euch verbringen konnte. Vielen Dank noch einmal, daß Du Dir so viel Zeit für mich genommen hast. Besonders gerne erinnere ich mich an das gute Essen, an die Fahrt nach Kent und an die Fahrten durch das abendliche London.

Liebe Glenis !

Erst _____ ich Dich anrufen, aber dann _____ mir _____, daß Du ja auch gerne Post _____.
Darum möchte ich Dir schreiben, wie gut es mir diesmal in London _____ _____. Besonders schön _____ das Wochenende, das ich mit Euch verbringen _____. Vielen Dank noch einmal, daß Du Dir so viel Zeit für mich _____ _____. Besonders gerne _____ ich mich an das gute Essen, an die Fahrt nach Kent und an die Fahrten durch das abendliche London.

3 Poetry — read a short poem. Write one yourself in a similar style or as a spoof.

4 *Photoroman* — with bubbles blanked out. In pairs, students re-write the story. As a cross-curricular activity and using IT the actual photos could also be produced by students.

5 Diary — each person writes a diary. Group has to guess the identity of the author of each diary.

Conclusion

What is important for students is that they are doing something new and different. The teacher needs to develop activities and strategies that exploit language known already, but in a different (preferably less transactional) context.

Any activity also needs to move the students on, so that they progress in their knowledge of grammar and vocabulary and in their awareness of their own thought processes. It should increase their awareness of the culture, geography and history of the target country. Above all, it should stimulate and motivate.

Students need the basic skills that will prepare them to talk and write on a wide variety of subjects, in different registers and style. As they begin their journey across the bridge from GCSE to 'A' level they need to be able to look ahead with confidence, knowing that they have knowledge which can be built on and added to along the way. It will be a journey of discovery as the culture and language open up before them. But ultimately they need to feel that the journey will be worthwhile and they will step onto the other bank as successful 'A' level students.

Chapter 2

Planning 'A' level topics to achieve continuity and progression

Tony Lonsdale

There are four aspects which are considered in the course of this chapter:

- Planning issues for post-GCSE continuity and progression.
- What the GCSE achiever brings to the 'A' level course.
- Establishing general principles for language teaching and learning post-GCSE.
- How general principles translate into specific practices.

Planning issues for post-GCSE continuity and progression

There are a number of what I believe to be non-negotiable statements about pre-16 and post-16 language learning which make the issue of continuity and progression one that 'A' level language teachers need to address.

- Changes in pre-16 language learning **must have** a dramatic impact on post-16 course planning.
- Pre-16 language learning is not the old 'O' level with some bits missing.
- 'A' level conventions and established practices may no longer be relevant or appropriate.
- 'Bridging' is not a short-term or short-phase strategy to bring GCSE achievers up to some notional (conventional) 'A' level starting point.
- We need to look beyond the conventional content-driven programme and to redefine the what, when, how and why of post-16, post-GCSE language teaching and learning.

The conventional design of topic-based 'A' level programmes has elements of continuity and progression which served the clientèle for which it was designed, viz the post-'O' level learner. The aim of 'A' level language teaching and learning, then, was very much to provide more of the same, to build on the skills and knowledge previously acquired and to extend these through regular practice within a linguistically and thematically more challenging topic-programme. Now, our post-GCSE programme is serving a new clientèle. The GCSE achiever is bringing different skills, different knowledge, different learning experiences to the 'A' level course.

What the GCSE achiever brings to the 'A' level course

I have summarised in the ten-point profile given below what I see to be the general characteristics of the GCSE achiever. He or she is a learner who:

- enjoys communicating in the foreign language;
- uses the spoken language effectively in structured tasks;
- is well-practised in conducting pairwork exchanges and role plays;
- responds positively to 'interactive' challenges;
- is used to reading comprehension with support questions in English;
- is used to clearly defined vocabulary lists;
- has had little practice in translating from the foreign language;
- has had little contact with foreign language 'readers';
- is used to letter-writing as the main written activity;
- has had little if any experience of analysing the foreign language.

Taken collectively, these characteristics support the claim that students embarking on an 'A' level language course are, first and foremost, communicators and language users, not linguists and language learners. And therein lies the planning challenge, since the fundamental aim of the 'A' level teaching and learning programme is to develop, from and through communication, linguistic skills, and to make of language users autonomous language learners. Thus, the conventional 'more of the same' content-driven and topic-based programme has to be redesigned to become a skills-based programme which achieves continuity and progression.

To achieve **continuity**, we need to identify and define **skills-based phases of learning**. And to achieve **progression**, we need to define and structure a route through from defined-topic-vocabulary-dependency-with-limited-operational-effectiveness to autonomous-independent-language-acquisition-for-transferable-linguistic-skills.

General principles for language teaching and learning post-GCSE

My starting-point in refashioning the 'A' level programme is to consider the conventional structure according to topic-units. The diagram below represents the first year language programme divided into a linear sequence of topic-based 'slots' — the sort of structure that was first 'formalised' in *Actualités françaises* and that has remained largely unchanged since.

A	B	C	D	E	F	G	H	I	J

If we take the two or three-week 'slot' that each of those blocks represents and consider an alternative, skills-based delivery, we can identify three divisions or 'sub-slots'.

By repeating that division across the topic-units, we can establish three phases of teaching and learning, and thus have a structure which enables us to plan and design our programme in terms of skills-based phases.

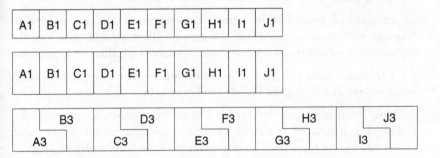

This revised structure provides a model which allows us to think of bridging not in terms of a short-phase 'leg-up' to 'A' level, but of a gradual transition over four phases (Year 12: Phases 1, 2 and 3; Year 13: Phase 4) into which continuity and progression can be more effectively incorporated. Thus:

Phase 1	builds upon	GCSE
Phase 2	builds upon	GCSE + Phase 1
Phase 3	builds upon	GCSE + Phase 1 + Phase 2
Phase 4	builds upon	GCSE + Phase 1 + Phase 2 + Phase 3

Chronologically, those Phases are organised in the following way:

Phase 1	First half-term of Year 12
Phase 2	Second and third half-terms of Year 12
Phase 3	Remainder of Year 12
Phase 4	Year 13

The Year 12 topic-based scheme of work is thus structured around three 'visits' to each of ten language topics and deals with these as a framework for developing language learning skills. The Year 13 topic-based programme I will come to later.

The general principles determining the design of each phase are set out in the sections that follow: each section also includes references to specific examples to illustrate the general principles.

Phase 1

The continuity element of Phase 1 is in 'tapping into' the communicative confidence and spoken language strengths of GCSE achievement, in sustaining the element of enjoyment in using the language communicatively, and in imitating GCSE-type tasks and activities in the context of 'A' level topics. The progression element can be identified as two-fold:

(a) an essential awareness in terms of language learning processes that language previously acquired and associated with a defined topic can be transferred to an unfamiliar topic-area and allow relevant, effective expression;

(b) a language skills progression in extending written expression beyond letter-writing and laying the foundation for awareness of accuracy.

A Phase 1 unit is designed to provide a short introduction to each topic by means of a structured communicative task managed by the teacher and performed by the students. The management of the task involves:

(a) preparing the stimulus material;
(b) preparing and rehearsing the linguistic requirements for the task;
(c) monitoring the performance of the task;
(d) leading the feedback after completion of the task;
(e) displaying language generated by the task and feedback;
(f) setting a written follow-up to the task as a homework assignment;
(g) monitoring the written assignment;
(h) following up the corrected written assignment.

In my scheme of work, the time-scale for a Phase 1 unit would be one lesson (1h15min) for (a) to (f) and one lesson for (g) and (h). In total, then, a Phase 1 unit occupies approximately 2h30min of contact-time.

Crucial to the success of a Phase 1 unit are the expectation that the teacher has of 'oral work' at this early stage in the course and the perception the teacher has of his or her role. In terms of expectation, it cannnot be over-emphasised that the Phase 1 introduction aims not to generate a *discussion* of 'A' level topics and issues, but rather to create the framework in which students will feel they can confidently *say something about* topics and issues. What they have to say may well be limited and impoverished: so be it. The teacher's role is to intervene at the preparation or feedback stage to extend and enrich those student-generated starting-points, to display all such language, and to ensure that all such language is noted by the students.

The materials which support Phase 1 tasks should be carefully selected: visual prompts or limited verbal prompts which encourage students to dig into their existing resources to make observations, offer information, elicit information, and so on, are by far the most effective; materials which are 'friendly' to users whose previous *modus operandi* in spoken expression has been strongly supported by English role play prompts or well-rehearsed personal information questions; materials which lend themselves to pre-16-type tasks and activities.

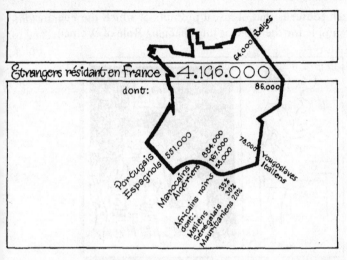

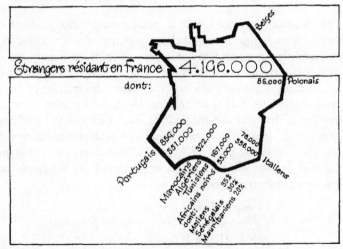

Statistical data (e.g. tables of results of opinion polls and surveys) are a ready-made stimulus for information-gap exchanges: the example taken from *Au courant* on the previous page has been adapted to the type of information exchange which students have previously conducted for timetable information. Preparation and rehearsal for this task would involve revising countries and nationalities; figures and statistics; the phrasing of questions needed to elicit information. The task would be performed through pairwork with the teacher circulating for 'quality control'. The feedback would concentrate on drawing conclusions, on stating observations, on feeding in 'expressions of quantity' and present tense statements and so 'drilling' structures which enable general observations to be made about the data given. There is no shortage of statistical data of this sort which can serve to introduce all manner of language topics in Phase 1.

An equally rich source is that of visual prompts of which the line-drawing below is an example for the topic of the Changing Role of Women.

The communicative task with a visual prompt, though more open than a pairwork exchange, is nonetheless structured. An invitation to brainstorm will doubtless produce familiar infinitives from the Family and Home topic (*faire le ménage; faire la cuisine; lire le journal; ranger les chambres*, etc). For the 'enrichment' conscious teacher, these are valid starting-points. The visual prompt gives the teacher the freedom to set the 'language-input' agenda. This may be to 'drill' the present tense of *faire*: it may be to 'drill' negatives *ne . . . pas/ne . . . jamais/ne . . . rien*. Displayed examples of statements generated can then serve to draw 'grammatical' observations. Or it may be that the teacher stays with the infinitive offerings from the group and feeds in a variety of link structures:

> *Le mari refuse de faire la vaisselle.*
> *La femme n'a pas le temps de lire le journal.*
> *Elle est obligée de faire la cuisine.*

providing these as 'models' to be imitated. Such a technique in itself has a GCSE 'continuity' and 'A' level 'progression' element about it in that the structures are similar to 'set-phrase' statements but are also transferable to other contexts. That transferability should be illustrated with reference to topics previously introduced:

> *Le gouvernement refuse d'aider les immigrés.*
> *Les immigrés sont obligés de vivre dans des foyers.*

'Transferred' statements of this sort can lead to investigative grammar work, i.e. what is the knock-on effect of changing one element in a statement?

The written follow-up assignment to the contact activity again emphasises the importance of realistic expectations at this stage: the students are required to do little more than a copying-up and tidying-up exercise with the language and structures they have noted. This 'low-key' written work is designed to target some of the very basics of written accuracy (correct spelling; correct accents; attention to details which may not have figured prominently in previous written expression). It is also an opportunity, in the follow-up stage, to focus on some of the essential 'un-learning' that is needed. It is a ground-rule in this phase that students operate within the language already acquired or noted in the lessons: dictionaries are banned!

By the end of Phase 1, students have an entry in their file for each of the ten topics. They have noted structures and vocabulary from the lessons, and for this I provide a vocabulary notebook. They have completed and have had marked ten short, written assignments and errors have been followed up in contact-time: these errors have been logged by students in a grammar log-book, with explanatory notes provided and further illustrations of relevant accurate points of language. This is an appropriate stage to shift the focus to effective study skills, to the importance of regular revision and review. The phased structure reinforces this principle: the material already on file for each topic will provide a point of access for the second phase, and thus teaching approaches reflect sound learning strategies. The end of Phase 1 is an opportunity to review with the group their perceptions on the differences between GCSE and 'A' level language learning, and on the basis of these, to establish a weekly schedule of independent study. The advantage of this over the start-of-course study-skills induction is that the discussion for students who are six weeks and ten topics 'down the line' is a better informed one.

Phase 2

The continuity element of Phase 2 is, obviously, afforded through the second 'visit' to Phase 1 themes and topics; there is also continuity of learning processes in the handling and application of foreign language skills. To this extent, Phase 2 represents 'more of the same': but the new direction, the progression element, is to be found in the sources and resources for learning. Phase 2 activities are based largely upon the processing of short written texts for language development and acquisition purposes.

In the model I am proposing in this presentation, those texts are almost exclusively written samples of language, and I feel some explanation for this is needed. The first point I would wish to make is that I am not convinced that all language learning should be 'delivered' through topic-based materials and tasks. For the teacher, it is an immensely time-consuming task to organise and edit out relevant 'topic-based' listening materials to incorporate into a totally topic-based programme. But, more importantly, I am not at all sure that such an approach is in the interests of learners. To adopt the rather narrow criterion of relevance to topics in selecting listening materials would mean that learners are not exposed to a whole wealth of authentic and relevant listening material such as international, national and local news items, advertisements, weather reports, public information announcements and so on, that is items of spoken language which do not readily fall into the chosen topic categories. There has to be the scope within the learning programme to include such non-topic work, to develop listening skills for their own sake rather than for the knowledge, information or awareness of topical issues figuring in the Year 12 programme. Furthermore, listening is, by its nature, more appropriate as an independently practised skill: my scheme of work thus includes, in contact-time, an introduction to independent listening techniques, a 'kick-start' to private study listening, after which I see my role as that of providing the materials for students to take their cassette away with them and of monitoring the progress they make through the listening skills programme.

Contact-time for Phase 2 topic-work is therefore given over to the study in class of printed texts. The key-feature of these texts is their brevity. 'A' level conventions dictate that we should aim for quantity of material: my own approach is to reverse that and place the emphasis on quality of exploitation. And this for two reasons. First, GCSE learning through reading is very much based on 'snippets' of language: to expect students to move directly from this to lengthy and condensed passages of text is unrealistic and, I believe, counter-productive. Secondly — and more fundamentally — we must be clear about the purpose that texts serve. There is a risk of over-stating their function as information-providers and so of over-emphasising the importance of the thematic or topic content of selected samples. Students draw their awareness and understanding of topics and issues dealt with in the course from sources other than the texts we use, and more often than not, from native language sources. Our primary purpose is to provide the tools with which students can operate in those contexts in the foreign language: thereafter, it may be that we have a broader, educational role in influencing the views and opinions held, or in better informing the views and opinions held. My argument is that we should ensure that a student can effectively articulate a biased view in the foreign language before we challenge that view. We must acknowledge that the vast majority of our learners are **maturing** rather than **mature,** and that the foreign language they master serves them in that process.

The general principle that applies in dealing with written texts in this phase is that we need to be aware and take account of the skill-level of the learners: they are not proficient linguists who, when processing a text, switch between comprehension mode and analysis mode with the same ease as the teacher. A written text for students is a mine-field of potential hurdles and obstacles: if they are presented with it from 'cold', it will make very little sense, and the less sense they make of it, the less willing they will be to 'follow' the teacher's direction in 'unlocking' the complexity of structures and lexis which, allegedly, explains the meaning. The teacher who, fifteen lines into the text and twenty minutes into the lesson, is enthusing about the subjunctive *puisse* after *à moins que* or the subordinate clause word-order after *obwohl,* may well have lost the majority of the audience several lines and minutes earlier because they had stumbled over the meaning of a 'new' word. Comprehension and analysis are two distinct 'processing' modes, and the teaching approach must reflect this.

One practical technique which helps reduce comprehension obstacles is to conduct a pre-reading exercise prior to the students' encountering the text: on the basis of a headline prompt or a visual stimulus accompanying or related to the text, the teacher invites the group to make predictions as to the content suggested by the prompt. In responding to the predictions, the teacher 'feeds in' language items that are contained in the eventual text: these may be lexical, structural, or indeed both. The purpose of these interventions is to familiarise the student with the otherwise unknown and/or difficult parts of the text so that a gist-reading can allow a gist-understanding, so that the student can process the general meaning of the text quickly and confidently, and so that a positive comprehension part of the study of the text will motivate the student to take a more detailed, analytical look at the language items selected for more 'in-depth' study. Clearly, for this preparatory stage to be effectively conducted, the teacher needs to be familiar with the text and to have considered any 'gist-comprehension difficulties' it may pose.

For the detailed analysis of the text, it is the linguistic rather than the thematic content that is more important. The way in which it is exploited will depend upon the purpose of the analysis: most teaching from texts, of this sort, is designed to 'deliver' grammar, and in the post-GCSE climate, the whole issue of grammar-teaching and learning has generated much discussion and debate. It is not within the scope of this presentation to examine this issue in any depth, but I would like to offer some practical strategies for approaching the teaching of grammar in the context of the skills-phases. First of all, I believe that students need to see grammar 'in action', i.e. they need to be able to look at and compare changing patterns in word and sentence structures or, as it were, the grammatical 'knock-on effects' of changing an element in a statement. Observation and comparison mean that grammatical awareness and knowledge can be gained and acquired more by investigation and less by spoon-feeding methods. Secondly, I would claim that there are effectively two 'types' of grammar for the foreign language learner viz the *productive* and the *receptive.* Grammar for productive purposes relates to points of language which learners need in order to operate effectively and accurately in spoken and written expression; grammar for receptive purposes is that which allows learners to interpret, decipher, translate and process language effectively and accurately. Conventionally, this distinction has not been made: grammar has been seen exclusively as a productive language tool. The distinction I have identified leads to a third practical strategy for approaching grammar which is that productive grammar lends itself more readily to 'communicative target-language' teaching whereas receptive grammar is more appropriately dealt with through independently completed worksheet exercises. And finally, the productive-receptive distinction addresses some of the problems of differentiation in grammar-learning in that the learners themselves will determine the pace at which receptive grammar transfers across into the productive grammar 'stock'.

Le rôle de la femme

Jacques, 25 ans, professeur, et sa femme Francine, 20 ans, sans profession, ont des idées très précises sur l'importance de partager les tâches ménagères.

Pour eux, l'homme doit être préparé à son rôle au foyer dès l'enfance, à l'école et surtout dans sa famille.

- De ce point de vue, explique Francine, la mère a une grande influence sur l'enfant. Ses préjugés, ses attitudes à elle déterminent en grande partie le comportement que le garçon aura plus tard vis-à-vis de la femme. C'est la mère qui, indirectement, apprend au fils à considérer (ou à ne pas considérer) la femme comme son égale.

- Prenons le cas de beaucoup de mes élèves, ajoute Jacques. Ils ne font pas leur lit, ils ne rangent pas leur chambre, parce que leur mère considère que ce n'est pas un travail d'homme. Il est certain que ces garçons, plus tard dans la vie, risqueront de traiter les femmes comme des esclaves. L'école a un grand rôle à jouer en changeant les attitudes traditionnelles.

- Pour nous, l'idée de partager est très importante, poursuit Francine. Beaucoup d'hommes pensent à aider leur femme seulement quand ils ont des enfants. Jacques et moi ne sommes pas de cet avis. On ne change pas en un instant comme ça. Vivre avec quelqu'un c'est tout partager . . . y compris la cuisine et la vaisselle!

Trente ans, dix ans de mariage, trois enfants . . . Depuis trois ans, Monique est secrétaire dans une société de produits chimiques. Avec son métier, ses enfants, son appartement, n'est-elle pas surchargée de travail ?

- Mon mari m'aide, explique-t-elle. Surtout depuis que je travaille. Luc et moi nous occupons ensemble du budget, du ménage, et de l'éducation des enfants.

- Il n'y a pas beaucoup de maris comme Luc !

- Mais si. Beaucoup de ménages s'organisent de la même façon. Il y a de moins en moins de domaines qui sont réservés à la femme et d'autres au mari. Cela tient au fait qu'il y a de plus en plus de femmes qui travaillent. Les conditions de vie changent, et avec cela les façons de se comporter. Chez nous, cela n'a posé aucun problème. Je sais que pour d'autres ménages, c'est plus difficile. Ils doivent peu à peu changer leurs habitudes : apprendre à organiser ensemble leur vie de chaque jour, à résoudre en commun les problèmes. Et pour certains, surtout dans les générations précédentes, ce n'est pas possible. Par exemple, ma mère s'étonne toujours quand elle voit Luc en train de passer l'aspirateur. Elle dit que mon père n'a jamais fait cela et n'aurait jamais accepté de le faire.

I should now like to give a flavour of how these general principles of Phase 2 translate into specific practices. Examples below are from the two texts given on the previous page.

Pre-reading exercise: the illustration from Phase 1 is adapted as a stimulus for feeding in language to assist gist reading of the two passages. The stereotype roles illustrated here are in sharp contrast to the content of both texts and the teacher could give *vrai/faux* prompt statements about the couple's attitudes towards or adherence to less traditional role models.

Through questions to the group the husband's attitude and behaviour can be tracked back to the role models to which he was exposed as a child:

> *Quand il était petit,   est-ce qu'il faisait son lit?*
> *est-ce qu'il rangeait sa chambre?*
> *A l'école, est-ce qu'on parlait de l'importance de partager les tâches ménagères?*

The Phase 1 stimulus is thus extended to bring in Phase 2 language and prepare the ground for reading.

Gist-comprehension: quick-fire questions on general points of information in the passage are a means of boosting the students' confidence in their gist-comprehension skills. If the pre-reading exercise has been effectively carried out, after the first reading the comprehension questions can usually be answered with the sheet of text turned over.

Analysis: for productive grammar purposes, from text A for example, I would have displayed on the OHP the paragraph beginning *Mon mari m'aide . . .*, and below that, the following:

> *Monique explique que son mari l'aide. Surtout depuis qu'elle travaille. Luc et elle s'occupent ensemble du budget, du ménage, et de l'éducation des enfants.*

These would be identified as Version 1 and Version 2. Orally, this would lead to drilling substitutions for the *nous occupons/s'occupent* elements, feeding in different infinitives to adapt to each context . . . *faire les courses; se lever; aller au supermarché; avoir les mêmes intérêts; partager les tâches ménagères,* etc.

Productive grammar exploitation aims to give students transferable structures and an understanding of how the transferred context or changed elements affect the pattern of the statement.

Analysis: for receptive grammar purposes introduces students to translation from the foreign language through selected examples which are then 'drilled' by means of a written exercise.

> *Elle dit que mon père n'aurait jamais accepté de passer l'aspirateur.*
> *Il dit qu'il n'aurait jamais accepté de travailler dans un bureau.*
> *Elle dit que son père aurait refusé de faire les courses.*
> *Je pense que beaucoup d'hommes dans les générations précédentes auraient protesté contre l'idée de partager les tâches ménagères.*

Receptive 'elements' drilled in this way, at this stage, form a useful source of language and examples of usage that can be referred to later when more 'complex' productive language is introduced. They are also useful as a menu of structures to which reference can be made, according to individual strengths, to improve a student's written style and quality of language.

Phase 3

The continuity element of Phase 3 is in the exploitation of topic-based materials for language acquisition and development and in speaking tasks devised around these; the progression element moves the learners forward in a number of ways. First, the length, range and complexity of samples of language studied address the need for linguistic and thematic progression. Secondly, the organisation of teaching and learning in this phase is such that greater responsibility is placed upon the learners through the use of Supported Self Study (SSS) units. Thirdly, the learning activities devised for the SSS units have an 'in-built' progression in that they begin with comprehension and language manipulation tasks based on the source materials and extend from these to composition-type outcomes involving the rehandling of ideas and language encountered in the units.

The general structure of the third phase of a topic is as follows:

1 'Starter' activity for the whole group

2 Sub-groups working on different SSS tasks

3 'Concluding' activity for the whole group

Notes:

1 The starter activity would draw on Phases 1 and 2 'visits' for general revision purposes and would then introduce the new direction(s) that Phase 3 provides. An appropriate text or video-clip might support this starter activity.

   This stage also deals with organisational matters i.e. what SSS units are available; how are sub-groups to be organised and arranged; who is doing what; deadlines for the first unit to be completed; negotiated learning.

2 The teacher circulates and spends time discussing with sub-groups the units they are working on: this review-work is conducted in the foreign language. It may be to 'correct' exercises already completed; it may be to discuss topic-related issues and ideas.

Sub-division of the group for spoken language practice is an essential management strategy in the case of large groups.

The range of tasks available for SSS addresses the issue of differentiation.

3 The 'concluding' activity provides the framework for students to report back on different tasks and activities; to present information to the rest of the group; to perform a role play prepared as part of an SSS unit, for example.

As with Phase 2, it is not intended that all teaching and learning is delivered through topic-based materials. There is the need for regular, dedicated 'grammar slots' in an 'A' level scheme of work either to present and practise new structures, or to revise and consolidate pre-'A' level points of language, and it is often more appropriate to take the overall range of topics rather than a single topic as the framework for such teaching and learning. The skills-based structure of phases of learning in Year 12 is intended not as a rigidly or exclusively topic-based programme but as one which affords the flexibility required to address a wide range of learning needs and requirements.

Phases 1, 2 and 3 are seen very much as a 'foundation' year in the two-year course, providing both the language-performance and language-learning skills which enable the second year — Phase 4 — to be organised more along 'conventional' lines. My only departure from convention in Phase 4 is to devise a programme based on **breadth** of themes and topics rather than on **depth**. 'A' level has tended in the past to try and make of learners experts and specialists with in-depth encyclopaedic knowledge and fully informed views on current affairs and issues, often at the expense of that versatility and linguistic resourcefulness which enable them to operate effectively across and within a whole range of topics and themes.

'A'

Part two

·

Using the language

Chapter 3

Grammar into creativity

Betty Hunt

In language teaching, we have become used to basing our lessons around topics, from personal details, at GCSE, to more demanding subjects for advanced students such as the environment, the generation gap, or violence. Authors of post-16 course books make sure that grammar work is spread evenly between the chosen themes and that there is progression from simple to more complicated structures. But if we use a more magpie approach to finding material or if we fail to complete the course book we risk selecting grammar in a random way and our students' knowledge can be incomplete. Aware of this possibility, some teachers compile a check list of grammar points and tick them off, others devote a few weeks to a crash course or crash courses, some address 'grammar needs' as they arise and others do all of these things.

Another idea is to add to our list some **grammar topics,** i.e. topics selected for their **grammatical** content and use them, when appropriate, to revise, practise or introduce the grammar we wish to teach.

Usually, we store texts in subject folders. Jacques Brel's song *Les vieux* (1963) would probably be filed under family or old age. After the pleasure of listening, the comprehension and the discussion we might exploit the language — the direct object pronouns perhaps:

*la pendule d'argent . . . qui dit, 'je **vous** attends'*
*qui **les** attend*
*qui dit 'je **t'**attends'*
*qui **nous** attend*

Or the negatives:

*et **n'**ont **plus** d'illusions et **n'**ont **qu'**un coeur pour deux*
*Les vieux ne rêvent **plus** . . . le muscat de dimanche **ne** les fait **plus** chanter.*

In a grammar topic, the grammar is the first priority and not the afterthought. Instead of building a theme round its content we select certain grammar points and devise a topic which will provide opportunities to teach them.

Devising a grammar topic

1. Select the grammar point

Each group has its own weaknesses; students may ask for help with certain points or the teacher may identify areas where practice is needed.

2. Context

What context will provide the opportunity to practise these points?

For the past tenses, the context could be storytelling.

For the passive voice, a collection of newspaper articles reporting road accidents or crime.

For adjectival agreements, descriptions of people, places and things.

For the imperative, articles from magazines: recipes, advice on dealing with adolescents, physical exercises . . .

For the conditional, choice of career and studies, *'si c'était à refaire . . .'*

3. Texts

Assemble material.

4. Activities

Choose a list of tasks which:

a gives a good balance of reading, listening, speaking and writing;
b includes communicative activities;
c suits the group's ability and interests;
d lasts as long as the time available but not so long that the group becomes thoroughly bored;
e helps students to become confident and accurate, progressing from simple tasks, to creative writing.

Teaching methods

1. Carousel

Initial presentation to whole class is followed by a list of activities and deadline for their completion. Individual students choose in what order to tackle tasks. There is no rigid pattern for such a carousel and no desirable length of time for a topic to be completed. Some tasks require whole class participation and some groups may find particular tasks difficult so that whole class teaching will be appropriate several times during the topic. Some material cannot be taken home but many tasks will be suitable for homework or the classroom.

2. Marking

a   Oral and written work can be assessed individually while the rest of the group gets on with chosen tasks.

b   The group can decide together how some tasks should be assessed: for example, how many marks out of twenty for accuracy, variety of language, intonation, pronunciation?

c   Lists of answers to straightforward written tasks can be available so that students mark their own work. They should consult the teacher when they have made mistakes and do not understand why their answers are wrong.

d   Encourage students to check other students' work for accuracy. When exploiting authentic material, write a list of answers; it is time consuming to do it later.

3. Target language

a   When examples are given, students soon recognise the essential vocabulary; the teacher can talk about '*les terminaisons*' while pointing to the verb endings on the transparency or on the board.[1]

b   A good source for mechanical written exercises and for the language needed when talking about grammar is the series of holiday homework books on sale for French children.[2] Some sections in textbooks intended for pupils in the French classroom are useful too.[3]

c   Teachers who fear that students will be afraid to say that they do not understand might like to allow a time towards the end of the lesson when students can ask questions and be answered in English. Usually, they are re-assured and can soon do without this safety net.

4. Reading aloud

The last session of a grammar topic should be handed over to the students so that they can read out their best work to the whole group and praise one another.

Examples of tasks taken from a grammar topic

Students need to revise the perfect tense and to be reminded of when to use the perfect and when to use the imperfect. The past historic might be entirely new to them. A topic based on storytelling provides ample opportunities for practice in these tenses. These are a few of the activities that might appear in such a topic.

Activities

1. Spread out a selection of postcards. Students choose three each. Giving them adequate preparation time, ask them to tell the class (or write) a story linking the three cards and using the past tenses. You can limit the number of sentences and be specific about which tenses should be used. Note the students' strengths and weaknesses and decide how much extra practice is needed.

2. Discuss the use of tenses in an extract from a narrative where the writer has used both the imperfect and the perfect, e.g. this passage from the last paragraph of *Musique à Gogo*, taken from a French page in *EG*, the education section of *The Guardian*.[4]

> **Jean Charles:** *Il y a trois ans, c'était ma première fête de la musique. Je suis sorti avec mon saxo sous le bras et j'ai rencontré un copain percussioniste. On s'est installés sur un banc à Montmartre et on s'est mis à improviser. Musicalement c'était nul mais on était contents de se retrouver.*

To draw the students' attention to the way the perfect tense is used for expressing a series of events and the imperfect to set the scene, copy the sentences again, using heavy print for the introductory 'scene setting' sentence and for the conclusion. Between the two, leave a space and then print the series of events as a list, emphasising each example of the perfect tense:

> *Il y a trois ans, c'**était** ma première fête de la musique.*
> *Je **suis sorti** avec mon saxo sous le bras,*
> *et j'**ai rencontré** un copain percussioniste*
> *on s'**est installés** sur un banc à Montmartre,*
> *et on s'**est mis** à improviser.*
> *Musicalement c'**était** nul, mais on **était** contents de se retrouver.*

After discussing the passage, various activities might be appropriate:

- translating
- changing some of the tenses and then translating again: *Je **sortais** avec mon saxo sous le bras et j'**ai rencontré**...*
- dictation
- IT (fun with texts)
- adding dialogue, more events, more description
- asking the students to apply the same technique of simple summary to a passage from another story or film. e.g. from *La dentellière:*[5]

> *Pomme passait ses vacances à Cabourg.*
> *Elle est entrée dans un café,*
> *s'est assise à une table*
> *et a pris une glace au chocolat.*
> *Elle était toute seule.*

or:

> *Aimery s'ennuyait.*
> *Il a vu Pomme,*
> *s'est assis près d'elle dans le café*
> *et lui a posé des questions.*
> *Il était content d'avoir trouvé cette jolie fille.*

3. For more work on the perfect or the imperfect tenses, either in class or at home, for the whole group or for selected students, use appropriate exercises from course books and grammar books, e.g. these exercises from *Atelier grammaire*:

Activité 1

En employant l'imparfait et le passé composé, faites des phrases pour décrire comment on a perdu une mauvaise habitude.

Exemple: Maintenant, je mange très rarement des bonbons.
Avant, je mangeais trop de bonbons entre les repas mais, un jour, j'ai eu très mal aux dents.

Maintenant:

1   *Elle ne sèche jamais les cours.*
2   *Il se lève de bonne heure.*
3   *Nous ne buvons que l'eau.*
4   *Tu ne te ronges plus les ongles.*
5   *Je dis toujours la vérité.*
6   *Ils roulent lentement*

Activité 2

Ask students to write twelve sentences describing the way they are now and the way they were ten years ago, e.g.

Je déteste aller à la piscine; il y a dix ans j'y allais toutes les semaines.

Give them the beginning of the present tense sentences:

Ecrivez des phrases pour faire votre portrait en commençant par:

1. je suis	4. j'ai	7. je vais	10. je déteste
2. je suis	5. je sais	8. je dois	11. je crois
3. j'ai	6. je sais	9. je crois	12. je pense

Changez les phrases, employant l'imparfait pour vous décrire il y a dix ans.

---

4. Listen to recordings of some of Prévert's poems [6] (made by an assistant?) and then study them; they should be chosen for the way they tell a story and for the use of the perfect tense, e.g.

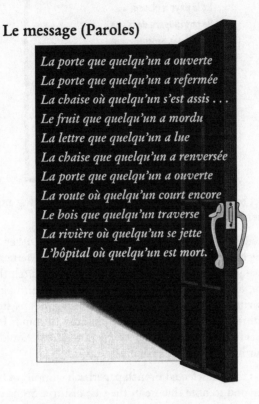

Le message (Paroles)

La porte que quelqu'un a ouverte
La porte que quelqu'un a refermée
La chaise où quelqu'un s'est assis . . .
Le fruit que quelqu'un a mordu
La lettre que quelqu'un a lue
La chaise que quelqu'un a renversée
La porte que quelqu'un a ouverte
La route où quelqu'un court encore
Le bois que quelqu'un traverse
La rivière où quelqu'un se jette
L'hôpital où quelqu'un est mort.

Some students might like to choose a poem and prepare a group recitation and accompanying mime. Guide the students in identifying certain aspects of Prévert's style: the pattern the poems make on the page, the use of uncomplicated language and the repetition and then ask them to write a poem, in the perfect tense, like the ones they have been reading but whose subject matter must be some event featured in the media during the past few weeks.

This poem was written by a student:

> Jamie
> Il a pris la main de deux inconnus
> Et le pays a pleuré
> Ils ont disparu de la vue
> Et le pays a pleuré
> Les forces de l'ordre se sont mobilisées
> Et le pays a pleuré
> Ses parents ont imploré son retour
> Et le pays a pleuré
> On a trouve son corps mortar
> Et le pays a pleuré
> Sa mort

It is not perfect but the student enjoyed the creative writing and wanted very much to do her best work.

5. Ask the students to work in pairs and to tell each other a story about themselves, the kind of stories which become part of the father of the bride's speech, i.e. the family legends. The students should then tell the group their partner's story, changing the first person narrative to third person and they should then write the stories (their own, this time), not as stories aimed at adults but with an audience of younger children in mind. Presentation is important; decide together whether word processors should be used and whether the anthology should have illustrations.

6. Ask students to read selected French paperback editions of books for very young children and to note the use of the past historic. Some pages could be discussed together. A good example is Bruno Heitz' *Ouah!, le chien écrivain* (Hachette, 1988), which, as the title indicates, is about a dog who wrote a book and managed to get it published: *Le premier éditeur lut le manuscrit à l'envers et lui conseilla de revoir la fin, et le début. Le deuxième regretta le manque de couleur et trouva le texte un peu court.*

Le troisième l'encouragea mais lui parla si bien de la crise du livre que le chien faillit pleurer ...

This task does not take very long; because of the lovely illustrations, the text quoted above takes up four pages.

I hope that these examples giving suggestions for teaching grammar will be of use to practising teachers.

References

1   A glossary of grammar terminology is given in *Atelier grammaire,* Hope M and B Hunt (Oxford University Press, 1993)

2   e.g. *Passeport nouveau pour le CM1* (Hachette, 1986), *Le verbe finissait est à l'imparfait*... *les noms féminins se terminent par*... *à quel temps est ce verbe?* ... *sera est le futur du verbe être*... *complétez les phrases en choisissant*...

3   e.g. Evelyne Amon and Yves Bomati, *Carnet Collège Brevet, Français 3e* (Hatier,1992)
Le participe passé employé avec avoir, s'accorde avec le complément d'objet direct (COD) si celui-ci est placé avant le verbe.
Tu m'as donné des pommes
avoir COD
Les pommes que tu m'as données.
nom fém. plur. COD avoir participe passé, fém. plur.
Accordez les participes passés des verbes mis entre parenthèses:
Q. *Les gâteaux qu'on leur avait (apporter), ils ne les avaient pas (manger).*
R. *Les gâteaux qu'on leur avait **apportés**, ils ne les avaient pas **mangés***

4   *The Guardian,* 27.6.95

5   *La Dentellière,* starring Isabelle Huppert and directed by Claude Goretta (1977) based on the novel by Pascal Lainé (Gallimard, 1974)

6   Jacques Prévert, *Paroles* (Editions Gallimard, 1972)

Chapter 4

A matter of discourse — ways of developing learner competence

Lid King

This is a short story. It is about teachers and learners. The teachers are unhappy — their learners cannot do enough. The learners are frustrated — they do not know enough. They know about objects. They can ask questions. They can talk about events. They can buy petrol. They can read stories. It is not enough. They want more.

One of the principal challenges of post-threshold teaching (typically post-GCSE, post-Standard Grade, NLS level 2) is to help the learner progress from familiarity with such simple (transactional or narrative) language to a deeper level of understanding and usage. This challenge is not new — there has always been a point at which second language learners have needed to progress from re-use of the simple and concrete ('assimilated chunks of language') to the representation of more complex and individual meanings. What is new is the context in which we now face up to this challenge.

The first context is everything that relates to the often quoted and equally often misunderstood 'Communicative approach'. Whether we relate this to the seminal work publicised in the Council of Europe Threshold Level (1970) or more recently to the introduction of new courses and forms of assessment (notably Graded Objectives and in most of the UK the languages GCSE) there is a palpable feeling that this has encouraged only superficial language competence. Learners, we are told, are better able to understand spoken language, they have an active vocabulary, they are able to 'get by' and yet . . .[1]

It is the 'and yet . . .' which this chapter will seek to address.

Secondly it must always be remembered that over the past 25 to 30 years the numbers of language learners in this country have increased dramatically, not necessarily at advanced level but certainly in the school 11–16 sector and in what are often (mis)called 'non-specialist' courses in higher education.[2] There should be little doubt that the essentially practical and realisable goals of initiatives such as Graded Objectives have been a great success and entirely appropriate in making language learning relevant and useful for this wide range of learners and needs.

Nor should we overstate the problem. Advanced language learners still make progress in this most challenging of disciplines, still manage to write and speak about literature, art, and the meaning of life in ways which are both individual and meaningful even to unsympathetic native speakers.

And yet . . .

That there is an issue is evinced not simply by the possibly subjective feelings of many thousands of teachers, but by the more objective evidence for example as collated by OFSTED. In the review of inspection findings for 1993/94 it is reported that:

The standard of listening comprehension was usually sound and often good . . . In the best cases . . . students displayed fluency in speaking and an ability to participate fully in discussions, arguing their point of view. **This contrasted with other cases in which students showed a lack of confidence in speaking: they appeared to understand the foreign language reasonably well but lacked the confidence to attempt more than short statements.** *These difficulties may have originated in an inadequate preparation at Key Stage 4. Students could usually understand . . . texts without difficulty and could write,* **although with variable accuracy** *on a range of topics. Whilst the best writing was impressive,* **some students struggled to cope with the increased demands of sixth form work.** (Our emphases.)

If more evidence were needed that this is something more than the nostalgic longing for a golden age — *in my day we did things better* — one need only look at such 'official' programmes and recommendations as the National Curriculum documentation and more recent work of the Council of Europe. In each case there is an explicit development from a purely functional (transactional) use of language to something more complex, abstract and individual.[3]

This is not to negate the value of functional language. It is simply to re-affirm that language is about more than buying bread alone; it is also about the other things by which we live — affirming individuality, negotiating meaning, interacting with others . . .

It would seem particularly appropriate that such mature and enlightening interaction should be a major objective of the sixteen-year-old language learner.

Language learning and discourse competence

These pages have no pretensions to theoretical originality. It is, in that respect, a rather typically Anglo-Saxon and empirical collection of 'useful and relevant ideas'. However all ideas have some starting point, conscious or not and if there is any coherence in what follows it resides in a certain view of second language learning within an institutional framework (as opposed, for example, to learning in the target country).

The first and most obvious thing to be said about this context is that it is extraordinarily difficult, and in many ways unpropitious for the flowering of such complex competencies and understanding. In this respect Professor Hawkins' description of the process as 'gardening in a gale' has never been bettered. This will have implications for how we address the issue.[4]

The second general point to be made derives from this very complexity. Language **learning** is not a single phenomenon. It involves a range of processes and activities and to be successful it requires the development of a similarly wide range of competencies. This appears to be more than the complexity which can be attributed to any field of learning — whether fishing or quantum mechanics, in that language learning involves not only the acquisition of new **skills, knowledge and lexis** (as do fishing and mechanics) but also a new **syntax** through which those skills, knowledge and lexis must be approached and without which they remain incoherent and primitive. In common with other kinds of learning, language learning also relies on our prior knowledge of the world. Again there is a key difference in that the world on which the new language is based may be culturally and historically quite unfamiliar and/or misleading.

Without labouring the point it is nonetheless likely that this unique complexity will have an effect on the learning process and our learners.

There are many ways of classifying the processes and competences involved in language learning, and it is unlikely that experts will ever agree on a common description. The most recent and probably the most comprehensive such attempt describes over twenty different competences divided into two main headings and seven sub-groups.

For our more modest purposes let us assume a simpler and less comprehensive framework. What kind of competences and knowledge are needed by our target group (post-16 intermediate language learners)?

Firstly and most obviously **Lexical knowledge.**

Without an adequate knowledge of vocabulary it is virtually impossible for learners to progress.

Secondly **Strategic competence.**

This may imply an ability to make sense of what is as yet unknown in the target language (without which ability the learner is continually frustrated) or more simply the ability to 'cope' and 'get by' with limited language.

Thirdly **Grammatical knowledge.**

Learners need to understand, internalise and re-use the systems of the language relating to number, gender, word order, syntax, etc.

Fourthly **Discourse competence.**

Learners also need to recognise and use key markers which denote a particular type of language and to develop language through appropriate links, subordination, etc. It is this competence in particular which delineates the independent user of language.

There are of course other kinds of knowledge which are relevant (for example knowledge of the world, the ability to learn (study skills) but these four general categories should suffice for our purposes.[5]

What is perhaps striking about these areas of knowledge or competence is not so much that they are interrelated — which is undoubtedly true — but the extent to which it has been possible to develop them **as discrete elements** of learning. It is at least arguable that the feelings of unease and frustration identified earlier arise because we have interpreted 'communicative methodology' in a way which has developed lexical knowledge and strategic competence **to the detriment of grammatical and discourse competence.**

A cursory review of language textbooks (especially from the 1980s) and the kind of tasks devised for Graded Objective schemes will show a preponderance of learning activities designed to help learners firstly to acquire relevant vocabulary and, secondly, to get across a message. In other words the stress has been on lexis and strategies (in its more limited sense).

The question therefore arises — what kind of activity or teaching framework will encourage those other necessary competences — Grammatical and particularly in this case Discourse competence?

Implications for teaching and learning

It has often been observed that language classrooms are relatively noisy places. There tends to be a great deal of activity — speaking, chanting, moving — and considerable interaction between pupils and pupils and pupils and teacher. Such activities, systematically organised, have undoubtedly contributed to the significant extension of communicative competence among many pupils.

They may also contain the seeds of a problem. For in order to develop discourse competence a different kind of interaction is also needed — interaction between the learner and the language (in the form of text, whether written or spoken). This may happen in the best organised classrooms, but evidence suggests that a great deal of what goes on involves repetition followed by re-use, with little intervening time for reflection. It is the reflection (interaction) which we need to promote. For this to happen there are three key conditions, which are also relevant to our learners well before they reach the age of sixteen.

Allow time

It takes time to internalise language, certainly to a degree where it can be re-used in a personal way. It may be that not enough time is devoted to assimilation/practice exercises, even in the early stages of learning — what Wendy Bromidge has referred to as the '50 ways' of using the same language. Given the overall constraints on our teaching time — and the difficulties of gardening in a gale — this may appear a 'waste of time'. On the contrary it is precisely because the young shoots are so fragile that we need to spend time on helping them take root. [6]

Play with language

Many of us have balked at the earnestness of functional language learning (*Not another puncture . . .*). This may be more than a question of what we do or do not find interesting. The need to use so-called 'authentic' resources may have meant that we have forgotten some of the most important ways in which language ability is developed — through manipulation and play. Language itself is a rich source of language work and even the least motivated and competent learners can enjoy and profit from the creation of language rhymes. One example that springs to mind is of a boys Spanish class in the North West where the writing of bilingual 'poems' actually induced the beginnings of linguistic understanding:

> *Yo me llamo Rudi Gullit*
> *I am faster than a bullet*

In other examples (preserved for posterity on a forthcoming CILT/St Martin's video) young pupils are given space to 're-use' slightly outrageous language is a way that personalises it:

> *Ah! Non, pas Tricolore. Ça pue.*

To avoid libel it must be stressed that this comment was no reflection on that excellent course. It merely meant that the pupils were seeking to express ways of saying that they did not want to do any work. The acceptability of play meant that they were able to manipulate and use language. [7]

Use prior knowledge

No learners come to us as empty slates. They have knowledge of the world and knowledge of language (*Why do you say l', Sir?*). Even beginners are full of questions which are often unanswered. We must find ways of harnessing that knowledge and enthusiasm into reflection about language and real interaction with text.

What follows are some suggestions about how we might do this.

Activities to help develop discourse competence

1   Explicit teaching of appropriate lexis

There is almost nothing new under the sun and learners have always been 'taught' discourse competence. The traditional vehicle for this teaching was the 'A' level essay:

> *'Necessity is the mother of invention'. Discuss.*

Approaches to this task have certainly included interaction with text, discussion (using prior knowledge) and detailed planning of less daunting paragraphs/components.

A more traditional method has been the learning of set phrases to be incorporated in the final text, using a range of specially prepared source books or the teacher's own suggestions.[8] It seems unlikely that many students actually learn much using such an essentially uncreative and non-interactive approach or that it leads to deep understanding.

At best they may acquire unassimilated chunks of language, not qualitatively different from their 'level one shopping vocabulary' which leads to such characteristic all purpose examination offerings as:

> *C'est une question fort difficile à résoudre. Il faut peser le pour et le contre et il y a toujours le revers de la médaille. Certains disent que . . .*

Even so, such an approach cannot be ruled out — it undoubtedly has a place, in particular for *aide mémoire* or revision purposes . . .

2   Use of written text as source

This is a more recent learning model, involving a development of the more traditional *explication de texte* for the purposes of acquiring re-usable language. Most contemporary textbooks are largely based on the model of text input followed by a number of exercise types, for example:

Comprehension questions (target language, multiple choice, true false)

Identification and explanation of language (lexis and grammar) through gap filling, searches, dictionary work

Re-use, e.g. picking out phrases and rewriting them in new contexts

The question to be asked is the extent to which such activities develop our students' active capacities for language use (as opposed to checking their understanding of the text in question). In other words to what extent do they enable our students to interact with the text.

Here is an example (non FL specific) of a typical text which could be appropriate for the kind of learner who is reading this book.

Any course of learning involves four obligatory factors: a learner, a goal, content and a process. The communicative approach is concerned to observe the principle of authenticity in regard to each of them. In other words, it is concerned that in every dimension the course of learning should be appropriate to the learner's needs, expectations and experience on the one hand and to the realities of communication in the target language community on the other.

Essentially an authentic text is a text that was created to fulfil some social purpose in the language community in which it was produced. Thus novels, poems, newspaper and magazine articles, handbooks and manuals, recipes and telephone directories are all examples of authentic texts; and so too are radio and television broadcasts and computer programmes. As far as language teaching is concerned, however, 'authentic text' has come to have a rather more limited meaning than this. Many attempts to implement the communicative approach have found no use for literary texts (sometimes this is entirely appropriate to the learners' needs, but often it reflects a prejudice against the study of literary texts as a hangover from the grammar-translation method); and even in the last quarter of the twentieth century the physical reality of most classrooms prohibits the frequent use of video or computer materials. Accordingly, when language teachers use the term 'authentic text' they often mean a piece of writing that originally appeared in a newspaper or magazine and is probably of ephemeral value and interest.

from Little D, S Devitt and D Singleton, *Learning foreign languages from authentic texts: theory and practice* (Authentik, 1989, reprint 1991)

Here is an activity which might help the teacher of this imaginary learner in approaching this text. Play the part of the teacher.

Task

1 How did you read the text? (in detail/skimmed/gave up/didn't bother)
2 Draw your own conclusions from the answer to 1.
3 Make up some activities for a learner approaching this text.
   a Comprehension
   b Language 'exploitation'
   c Re-use
4 Draw some conclusions from your answers to 3.
5 What kind of activities will help develop Discourse Competence as we have defined it?

Comments

Since this is a genuine interchange (at a distance), it is highly unlikely that one will anticipate the reader/teacher's detailed response (even if there is one). Past experience and interaction with real rather than virtual readers nonetheless suggests that a number of points/conclusions might emerge.

1 Complex written text (even in your own language) is a difficult medium for learning. The learner easily becomes: bored, daunted, sidetracked, unsure of point, other?

2 Comprehension questions and answers demonstrate very little. The activity focuses learners' attention on what they think the teacher wants to know, rather than on real exchanges of meaning, e.g.
   Q. *What is an authentic text?*
   A. *It is a text that was created to fulfil some social purpose in the language community in which it was produced.*
   Learning =?

3 'Linguistic exploitation' exercises may have similar drawbacks:

   e.g. Substitute these phrases for phrases in the text:
   for some social reason
   In relation to language teaching, etc.

   The correct answer is the whole point.

4 Real interaction takes place when there is 'A' level of engagement by the learner — real interest, curiosity, competitiveness.

Despite the difficulties inherent in the use of written text for interaction — and this particular text was not selected with sixteen- to nineteen-year-olds in mind — it remains nonetheless a key medium for developing discourse (and grammatical) competence. Only by engaging with text, deconstructing it and then recreating new language will the learner really progress. It is, however, unlikely that such competence will develop spontaneously in any but the most able. The role of the teacher thus becomes that of providing conditions which encourage learners to engage with text and developing activities which help them to do so successfully.

In this it would be imprudent as well as impossible to be prescriptive — learning takes place in specific contexts and set recipes are therefore inappropriate. There are, however, some likely preconditions relevant to our example:

Firstly the key basis for learner/text interaction is likely to involve **interest** and **use of prior knowledge**. Our task should be to create the conditions for engagement on the part of the learner. This may happen because the text is an appropriate one for given learners (or even better if the learners have a say in choosing it). It is also likely to develop because the teacher has specifically aroused the curiosity or interest of the learners, perhaps with a picture or a song or quite simply in the example given by first asking them (the language teachers) to explain what a course of learning involves and to define an authentic text.

This reliance on the learners' **prior knowledge** and **interests** creates an immediate **dialectic** with the text. Once you have defined your own views — perhaps in discussion with others — the next step is to **compare** with the views expressed in the text.

This process of comparison based on interest brings us to the second key condition for developing our learners' discourse competence — the need for manipulation (**deconstruction, construction** and **acquisition**) of new language.

Through comparison of 'my/our ideas' with 'the text's ideas', detailed language work can be developed. This may involve many of the 'traditional' exercises alluded to above — sorting, listing, substituting for example — but placed in a clearer and more meaningful context. Key, however, will be the reduction of the argument to its essentials — the removal of all links, all redundancy. Significantly such a process can lead the learner precisely to identify those parts of the language with which we are concerned — the discourse markers. It is those 'non-essentials' (*is concerned to, in regard to, in other words, on the one hand, on the other*) which give this text shape and force — which make it a convincing argument. It is this language which is 'abstracted' in our 'A' level essay example and which we seek to help our learners to acquire in meaningful interaction. By removing it — for the sake of the comparison — they are actually identifying it for future use.

It is incidentally this 'discourse language' which is missing from the first paragraph of the current chapter, and which a curious learner might be induced to replace!

3   Speculation — prior knowledge/interacting with text

Another approach, also using written text but in this case with minimal textual input and even greater reliance on the learner and his/her curiosity is exemplified by the exercise which has become known as the 'dead man's pocket'. As with many good ideas it has an uncertain origin. We first heard of it in Jean-Louis Malandain's work on the *'papier authentic (que?) brut'* [9] but it seems likely that many others have an equal claim to the idea — fortunately there is no copyright.

The basic idea is as follows:

A collection of apparently random items are discovered in a dead man's pocket (or dead woman's handbag — there is no prejudice involved). The learners (best in groups) speculate and then produce an explication/account of his or her last few days.

The reader is of course at liberty to use and adapt this idea. It might first, however, be appropriate to hypothesise about the ways in which such an apparently simple activity helps develop discourse competence.

Firstly there is an intriguing context. Learners are not quite sure where all this will lead. It is a little risqué. Handled well there is **engagement.**

Secondly a situation has been created (not always easy) which provides an authentic context for the use of a certain kind of language — speculation, hypothesising:

I think that . . .   *It seems to me . . .*   *Maybe . . .*

and disagreeing, rejecting ideas:

No, that's not very likely.
Why not?

If such language is not available for use then there is an equally strong reason for learning it!

Thirdly the outcome demands the re-using of language in interesting and creative ways. Most learners take up the challenge, in particular if there is a possible link between the material and the teacher, to develop ever more complex and imaginative narratives and accompanying arguments.

In sum a quite different context has been used to develop interaction between learner and text, involving use of what the learner already knows, collaboration between learners and detailed consideration of appropriate language. This is of course just one example and it is to be expected that many more similar ones could be added by our hopefully interested but necessarily distant readers.

One obvious advantage of the 'dead man's pocket' is its ease of preparation and its immediate accessibility (compared with a more standard 'journalistic' or 'academic' text. This might suggest that there are other — even more accessible — routes to discourse competence, such as song, spoken language and video.

| 4 | Songs as a source for interaction — transcoding & hypothesising |

If one of the key ways in which we will help learners to develop discourse competence is through enabling them to interact with text, then the use of song as text type has a number of advantages. There is the obvious one of interest — a well chosen song-text will provoke the initial enthusiasm or curiosity (even in a negative sense) which we have already seen to be so vital as a precondition for real interaction. Perhaps more fundamentally the text of a song (as of a poem) tends to be tightly controlled and often repetitive — it is thus very suitable as a source type for the kind of deconstruction and re-use which we have been considering. This is particularly relevant in the case of the less experienced learner for whom exposure to large amounts of written text can be so daunting.

Readers will no doubt have their own ways of using songs in the language classroom, and it is likely that these existing approaches already help in the development of discourse competence (or can easily be adapted so to do). Here we simply outline two possible uses of song which seem relevant, one involving transcoding (from and between spoken, sung and written language) and the other involving the learners in hypothesising (and then comparing their hypotheses with the real version)

The *Capitaine abandonné*

The first example derives from some work done by one of the EFL Pilgrim's team — Gerry Kenny.[10]

The outline lesson (actually lessons) worked something like this:

Demonstration lesson

Participants were given the chance to experience the passage from organisation to development for themselves via a 35-minute French lesson using all four skills. Six people acted as observers during the lesson; no specific task was given to them other than to watch and give their comments at the end.

1. A text was shown on the overhead projector. Participants were asked to copy it down and, as they finished each line, to underline all the words they understood.

2. Each person calculated the number of words they had understood as a percentage of the total text. These scores were called out and traced on a line:

    0% ------------------- 100%

Results ranged from 97–100 per cent. Up to this point all work had been individual and involved no interaction, so the next instruction was for people to use all means at their disposal to get everyone's score up to 100 per cent.

This led to a peer-teaching phase lasting three to four minutes, after which 100 per cent scores were confirmed.

3. The group was told that their text was, in fact, the text of a song. They were invited to listen to the song on tape while following the words carefully.

After hearing two to three lines of the song, people realised that the text was jumbled (even though stages 1 and 2 had not revealed this), so the tape was stopped and rewound. Instructions were given to listen again, numbering lines.

This second listening revealed the correct order of lines of the song; this was then confirmed collectively on the OHP text where each line was numbered accordingly.

However, this listening also led to the discovery that the chorus of the song was missing from the jumbled text. For the third listening phase, people were asked to listen to the chorus again and note down or try to remember whatever snatches they could. After three playings and much discussion, a partial version of the chorus had been written on the board; at this point the teacher completed the blanks in the text.

4. The group now had a full version of the text of the song *Capitaine abandonné* by the French group Gold (WEA Records, 1985). Attention was drawn to the personal pronouns in the text, *ils* and *tu*. We brainstormed characters which we thought these could refer to, based on comprehension work done on the text. Five main ideas emerged:

ils des vieux marins
des capitaines abandonnés
l'équipe de football anglaise

tu l'auditeur
la petite amie de l'auteur

Working individually, participants chose one of these characters and wrote down five questions they would like to ask them. Instructions were to put questions in the second person, using the *tu* or *vous* form.

5. As questions were ready, people were moved into pairs for interviews using their questions: each person took it in turns to tell their partner who their five questions were for, and then put these to them one by one for their partner to answer spontaneously as that character. Some people worked quickly at this and were able to change partners and repeat the process at least once.

6. People returned to their places and were invited to write down a one-sentence personal conclusion/comment/thought about the song or theme of the song. The activity ended with several participants volunteering to read their sentences to the whole group.

from *Graded Objectives and the National Curriculum* (CILT, 1991)

In this example the song used was a French one. We have also worked it equally successfully with such English (actually Irish) songs as the following:

1) Written version

Sleep lay me down, you'll be there by my side

Please promise me

That when I wake up from my dreams hold me closely in your arms

And I will close my eyes

Love if you say you won't slip away

Then I won't rest until

I can go dreaming of forever more

2) Actual song

Sleep lay me down, hold me closely in your arms

And I will close my eyes

Please promise me that when I wake up from my dreams

You'll be there by my side.

Chorus: Love if you say, you won't slip away

Then I can go dreaming of forever more.

But I won't rest until

I know that you'll be here in the morning

by my side .

(Dan Seals, R Vanhoy, with additional lyrics by Charlie McGettigan) Chappell Music

The fact that the written version is grammatically acceptable (correct) but somehow 'not quite right' is actually critical to the exercise. It enables our learners to progress from a feeling or sense that 'they understand the words but don't know what it means' to a more explicit understanding of how discourse markers actually contribute to the 'making sense' of language. What also appears significant about the processes involved here is that the learner is fully engaged on the language itself, partly because he or she is having to swap codes (copying written version — listening to heard version) and partly because there is a mismatch between the two. There is, if you like, a linguistic problem to solve and an intrinsic reason for doing so (which brings us back to curiosity and interest).

Another day in paradise

Another useful approach which represents a simpler form of the text preparation described above has been that of introducing a song with a guessing game (questions from learners or teacher depending on level, custom and purpose). The example quoted is in English (*Another day in paradise* by Phil Collins), but it works equally well with any appropriate song-text.

Example — Yes/No answers only (like 20 Questions)	
Question/Guess	**Answer**
Is it/ It's about a man	YES
It's about a woman	YES
It's about children	NO
It's about animals	NO
Just one man and one woman	YES (probably)
Pause	

	(prompt)	Where are they?
Are they/they're at home		NO
On holiday		NO
At work		Not exactly
They're in town		YES
They are in love		NO
Pause		
		Do they know each other?
They are friends		NO
Strangers		YES

And so on until the essence of the 'story' is reconstructed, or as often happens in this particular case guessed. A narrative can then be established and compared to the original version which is then (and only then) heard. The text has actually been constructed, apparently out of the air. Again — as with the Dead Man's Pocket — opportunities have been provided for hypothesising — the rather bald question and answer session suggested above might be developed with *I think, It seems,* etc. In addition the possibility has been created for detailed comparison of 'learner/teacher generated' text and authentic (in this case song) text.

5   Bringing it all together — a multi-media approach

Just as song can be an appropriate medium for promoting interaction and reflection in our learners so too can an even more comprehensible source of language — the visual text. Here again the ideas which follow are not new, and we are indebted particularly to Anny King of the Cambridge University Language Centre for her work with visual texts. [11] Unlike the complex written text (Example 2) the visual text does not require linguistic understanding **before** its meaning is unlocked. Paradoxically it is this immediate access to content which can enable learners to concentrate on (interact with) the actual form and structure of the language. In this respect it is regrettable that much of our enthusiasm for video, television and satellite has been as a support for comprehension skills alone.

Of course video is rarely used in isolation from other sources of language and the following example shows how — in combination with a range of media — an authentic video extract was a powerful stimulus for the development of discourse competence.

The objective — with a real class of students — was to engage the learner's interest and develop their language skills using a range of authentic sources relating to the topic of the Environment (in this case the language was French).

The sources included:

- various advertisements on the dangers of pollution;
- a song by Jean Ferrat;
- a brochure on the sources of pollution;
- a video from the Frenchn television news on pollution in the Loire;
- a soundtrack of the video.

The project was developed over a number of lessons and home assignments and involved such traditional elements as:

- presentation and discussion of the theme;
- vocabulary listing, learning and testing;
- writing of discursive paragraphs on the theme.

Perhaps less traditional was the teacher's insistence on learner participation in all of these activities (even the vocabulary listing and testing was controlled by the learners), and the main mode of operation which was in groups of four or five. After the initial brainstorm each group tackled a number of tasks using the different sources and produced one or two of a choice of outcomes (radio interview, poster, article for example).

The visual text was a vital part of the process and despite its inherent linguistic difficulty most of the group were able to interact with it. Firstly they watched it without sound a number of times and were invited to predict the content. Secondly they were asked to predict the language of the extract — involving discussion, use of dictionaries and interchange with the teacher. Having produced their 'own' text they then heard and compared the real text.

Such detailed language work, which is described more fully elsewhere [12] certainly produced outcomes (in a good but not exceptional group of learners) which suggest a development of the kind of competences which have concerned us and which are the justification for this chapter.

La pollution – qui est responsable?

On pollue l'eau avec le pétrole et les égouts et l'air avec la fumée et le gaspillage toxique. La pollution est un grand problème pour le monde. Beaucoup d'usines emploient des chimiques produits. Jls polluent l'air et les voitures aussi. Jl ne faut pas employer l'essence de plomb, le monde a peur. C'est beau l'environnement.

Tout le monde est responsable, le malheur des hommes, les plages noires de pétrole et les pluies acides. Jl faut que ça s'arrête.

Although not a perfect — or indeed exceptional — example of French prose there is a degree of appropriateness of language (use of links and subordination) which is often missing from students of even greater maturity. This is particularly striking when one realises that the group in question was a class of 28 fourteen- to fifteen-year-olds in an ordinary comprehensive school.

Conclusion

The last example suggests one obvious conclusion — that we should not wait until the sixth form to develop discourse competence (or grammatical competence since the two are so closely related). Learning **about** language — in an appropriate and meaningful way — can be part of our learners' experience from a very early stage. It seems likely that the more we are able to foster such understanding among younger learners then the easier should be the transition to advanced work.

At the same time there does appear to be a particular need for post-threshold learners to acquire the more developed linguistic skills which this chapter has been considering. However many 'good ideas' we may have for helping them to do this, there seem to be two particular conditions with which we began and which have run like a thread through the examples we have quoted. It will be as well to end with them:

- such competence needs **time**. Time for learners to process language (comparing, sorting, playing). This is not **wasted time;**
- in order for learners to develop their own language they must **interact** with language — not understand, 'go through', or repeat but **interact.**

Time and interaction will therefore be our final keywords. There will undoubtedly be many other approaches, methods and media — not least the possibilities offered by new technology (CD-ROM and telematics in particular) — but it is hard to envisage a process leading to successful language acquisition and use which does not involve both of these.

Given time we may therefore hope that the imaginary teachers and learners with whom we began our story will continue to learn together, developing the range of knowledge and skills which they both want and need. In so doing may they leave behind their unhappiness and frustration and live happily and interactively ever after.

References

1   Van Ek J A and J L M Trim (eds), *Across the threshold* (Pergamon Press, 1984)
    Page B and D Hewett, *Languages step by step* (CILT 1987)

2   James Coleman and Gareth Thomas in Hawkins E (ed), *30 years of language teaching* (CILT, 1996)

3 See for example National Curriculum Modern Foreign Languages
   Working Group I, *Initial advice:* 124–144 (DES/WO 1990)
   Also — *Modern foreign languages for ages 11–16:* 35 (DES/WO 1990)

4 Hawkins E, *Modern languages in the curriculum* (CUP, 1981)

5 See Johnstone R, *Communicative interaction: a guide for language teachers*
   (CILT, 1989) for a helpful description of learner competences

6 Bromidge W and J Burch, *In focus* video (CILT, 1993)

7 Burch J, *Opening the door on the languages classroom* (CILT, forthcoming
   1997)

8 For example:
   Hares R and G Elliott, *Compo! 2000* (Hodder and Stoughton, 1986)
   Horsfall P, *Advanced French vocabulary* (Mary Glasgow, 1994)
   Humberstone P, *Mot à mot* (Hodder and Stoughton, 1996)
   Ordo I M, *Advanced Spanish vocabulary* (Mary Glasgow, 1995)
   Stocker P, *Wort für Wort* (Hodder and Stoughton, 1996)
   Vigner G, *Ecrire et convaincre* (Hachette, 1975)

9 Malandain J L, *Le document brut aléatoire: le papier* (BELC, 1988)

10 King L (ed), *Graded objectives and the National Curriculum:* 39–40 (CILT,
   1991)

11 See in particular King A, *French means business* (BBC, 1993)

12 Page B, *Letting go, taking hold:* 39–40 (CILT, 1992)

'A'

Part three

·

Knowing the culture

Chapter 5

Communicating culture — approaches to teaching about German re-unification

Jim Anderson

On one level it is a fact that on 3rd October 1990 the Eastern and Western parts of Germany were re-united. This is without doubt an 'objective' reality defined in time and place and expressed in law. But there are other realities and the jumble of words and phrases below are signposts to some of these other realities.

Wende   Teilung -. Wiedervereinigung   Berlin

Mauer   **DDR - BRD**   Checkpoint Charlie

NBL - ABL   Sozialismus – Kapitalismus   SED

Diktatur – Demokratie   Honecker - Kohl   Stasi

Spitzel   Trabi   Plattenbau   Neues Forum

Goethe   **Arbeitslosigkeit**   'Tal der Ahnungslosen'

die friedliche Revolution   Wendehals   Bitterfeld

Besserwessi   FDJ   *Bach*   Aufschwung Ost

Umbenennung (Karl-Marx Stadt ➤ Chemnitz)   **PDS**

Sanierung   Korruption   Ausländerfeindlichkeit

Leipzig   **Ostalgie**   Frauenemanzipation   Weimar

Treuhandanstalt   Identitätsverlust   Dresden

Kriminalität   **Reisefieber**   Tag der deutschen Einheit

They serve on the one hand to remind us that there can be different dimensions to events (political, economic, social, etc) and different perspectives on them (East German/West German, employed/unemployed, young/old, male/female, resident population/'Ausländer', etc). On the other hand they demonstrate the complexity of what I shall argue to be the cultural component of language learning at 'A' level.

The term 'culture' is, in other words, being used here in a broad sense, which looks at how people relate to and experience the events and structures which shape their lives (i.e. an anthropological view) rather than focusing solely on 'formal culture' — the important dates, the famous people, culture with a capital 'C'.

What these words and phrases also show us is that language is an expression of culture and cannot be separated from it. Although 'Mauer' can be translated into English as 'wall' and although there is an area of common meaning between the two words, the connotations that the words carry for a German and a British person are quite different both in quality and intensity. Learning a language is in a quite fundamental sense learning to recognise and to understand another view of the world. The good student of language therefore is also a student of culture.

I shall attempt firstly to present a rationale for a consistent and clearly worked out integration of culture and language in 'A' level teaching and secondly to indicate a range of approaches of particular relevance in tackling the complex area of German re-unification.

Establishing aims and content — what's appropriate? What's realistic?

One of the problems in building the cultural component into teaching plans has been a vagueness about aims and a failure to take on board the extremely limited knowledge and understanding that many students have about both their own and the target cultures on entering the sixth form. Certainly the GCSE course should develop an awareness of differences in some areas of everyday life — the home, eating and drinking habits, school systems, public transport, etc — as well as of the appropriate form of language to use in different social situations. However, there is no coherent framework for teaching about culture nor any precise indication of the cultural knowledge and understandings that students might be expected to acquire. The result of this is that many students entering the sixth form lack even the most fundamental insights into the target culture.

Moreover, even if they have spent some time in a German speaking country on school trips or family holidays one has to be aware that attitudes towards Germany and the Germans in this country still derive to a large extent from media images centred on World War II. Such influence is of course insidious operating as it does at a sub-conscious level.

So where to start? We need to be clear firstly about what our aims are. Having described the overall goals of cultural teaching as *cross-cultural under-standing and cross-cultural communication*, Dr H H Stern in his book *Issues and options in language teaching* [1] summarises three main areas of focus identified in the literature. These are:

1. Cognitive goals

knowledge about the target culture, awareness of its characteristics and of differences between the target culture and the learner's own culture; and a research-minded outlook, i.e. willingness to find out, to analyse, synthesize, and generalize. Also . . . an emphasis on understanding the sociocultural implications of language and language use

2. Affective goals

. . . interest, intellectual curiosity, and empathy

3. Behavioural goals

. . . students should be able to interpret culturally relevant behaviour . . . and they should have the ability to conduct themselves in culturally appropriate ways

Stern goes on to point out that *Culture teaching, according to this conception, is less skill-oriented than it is problem-oriented, fact-finding, and evaluative* and that language teachers, not having been trained in the use of these techniques to teach culture, may in fact lack the necessary expertise to do so effectively. Coupled with this is the issue of whether all culture teaching at this level should be conducted through the target language. Given both the interrelationship between language and culture and the importance of 'message oriented' language use in promoting communicative competence it is clear that this should be the aim. It can only be achieved, however, with very thorough preparation and the use of appropriate teaching techniques.

With regard to content, Byram and Morgan [2] provide two helpful lists outlining firstly broad areas of study and secondly how these broad areas translate into themes and topics in German. In relation to German re-unification the most immediately relevant areas amongst those suggested are 'national history', 'social identity and social groups' and 'stereotypes and national identity'.

It is important to realise, however, that Byram and Morgan's lists are intended to provide a broad framework to assist the teacher in building an appropriate and balanced cultural component into schemes of work. It is not imagined that every aspect will be covered and certainly not in the kind of depth which might be expected of the specialist academic. Byram and Morgan, in fact, emphasise that language and culture courses are not courses in history, sociology or geography, but that . . . *it is the perceptions and knowledge of insiders about their own culture which frame the selection and the perspective from which content is presented'*. As they put it . . . *the aim is to provide learners with 'beacons' by which they can orientate to the behaviour, talk and texts they meet in the foreign environment.* The important thing is that students gain *an understanding of the significance of particular periods of history or social institutions or geographical facts in the understanding the foreign group has of itself and its identity. These can then be compared and contrasted with the learners' own national views of themselves and their identity and, through confrontation, a process of shift in perspective begun.*

The emphasis, in other words, is less on teaching students about culture and more on teaching them how to interact with culture. Being a good student of culture, therefore, means both looking outwards and looking inwards. It means taking account of one's own perspective and recognising that one's own view of another country is determined by a range of factors in one's own education, experience and personality. Where one is coming from crucially affects how one sees things. The point is well illustrated in the cartoon below taken from the journal *Fremdsprache Deutsch*.

Methodological principles

It is clear that, if we are to go beyond the superficial in teaching about culture and to provide students with the tools they need to explore the nature of their relationship with other peoples and other ways of life, then we need a methodology which stresses personal involvement and fosters a sensitive, open-minded, critical attitude. Some key principles upon which such a methodology might be based are as follows:

1 Integrating language and culture teaching across the four skills (moving from developing understanding to expressing opinion, i.e. from the receptive to the productive).

2 Building from the students' level of knowledge and understanding.

3 Generating interest and involvement through co-operative learning tasks.

4 Emphasising the ways in which external events (historical, economic, social, etc) affect individual lives including those of young people.

5 Exploring issues from different perspectives (or 'multi-perspectival realism', as Byram and Morgan[2] refer to it).

6 Fostering resourcefulness and independence through personal research (school-based or in German speaking countries)

7 Bringing issues alive through analysis of first-hand evidence (photographs, maps, reports, articles, songs, poems)

8 Reflecting the multi-cultural nature of German and British society as well as a wider international perspective

Techniques for teaching culture

Having outlined how we might, in theory, like to approach the teaching of culture, it is time to return to the topic of German re-unification and to try to identify a range of techniques which will enable us to put these ideas into practice.

There is a vast amount of material available for teaching about German re-unification. A selection of these titles, as well as ones relating to the teaching of cultural awareness in general are provided at the end of this chapter.

It should also be pointed out that the following techniques are those considered most appropriate for tackling this topic and are in no way intended to be exhaustive. The techniques are divided into six broad groupings. These are:

- Building an historical framework
- Exploring words and concepts
- Recognising points of view
- Carrying out research
- Forming and expressing opinions
- Interpreting and creating

Building an historical framework

1. Summarising

The booklet *Wende '89 – von der DDR zu den fünf neuen Ländern*[3] provides a clear twenty-page account of events leading up to re-unification which is useful background for students. With this, or any similar material, students, individually or in pairs, can be asked to prepare a summary of different sections of the text in German. This can then be presented to the rest of the group. This is good preparation for the very similar task set by at least one 'A' level examination board where students have to summarise an article from the British press in German.

2. Reading comprehension using a variety of text types and realia

(*Kleine Deutschlandkunde* [4]: 10–13)

Tasks can be based on various texts and documents which present a historical perspective (maps and photographs, a stamp, personal statements made by young people).

Such material help students to visualise the extent to which Germany has changed over a period of time. They also help to make the accompanying text more accessible.

This particular text is written in simple German with key words highlighted to assist note-taking. This is not to say that everything in it would be readily understood. Some key concepts that the teacher might need to elucidate include, for example, *der erste demokratische Staat, der Nationalsozialismus, die Diktatur Hitlers/eine Diktatur der SED.* Students are expected to study the documents and texts and then to answer questions in German which are given at the back of the book.

This approach enables students to familiarise themselves rapidly with a broad historical framework within which German re-unification can be situated and which allows them to some degree to appreciate its significance.

3. Culture flowchart

This is a very useful means of establishing the sequence of events in a historical process. Having established that students are familiar with how flowcharts work, the class is divided into groups and each group is given a set of flowchart-item cards. The groups are asked to put them into the right order and then to explain their ordering to the whole class.

(*Cultural awareness* [5]: 143)

4. Sequencing historical events

(Mary Glasgow Publications Factsheet: *Kultur Borgen,* 1990)

Once students have absorbed the most important information about the stages towards German re-unification, they can be asked either individually or in pairs to do a sequencing task.

This involves matching information about events to the dates when they occurred and helps students to take a longer term view of historical processes.

5. Video commentary

Either students first watch a video with sound (in German or English) and then watch it in sections without sound during or after which they provide their own commentary in German.

Or they see a video without sound and provide their own commentary after which this is compared with the real commentary.

Exploring words and concepts

6. Brainstorming

This is a valuable means of ascertaining what students know as well as high-lighting key concepts to do with the topic.

The teacher writes focus for activity (i.e topic heading or key concept) in the centre of the board/OHT.

Students working in pairs/groups think of ideas/associations and then feed back to rest of group.

7. 'Mental map'

This is a variation of the brainstorming idea. Students are given a blank map of Germany and asked to label and illustrate it in such a way as to reflect their personal image of Germany.

(*Typisch deutsch?* [6]: 96)

8. Comparative connotations

Students are given an English word, e.g. *border* or *wall* and asked to make a scattergram showing all the associations that the word has for them, with those that occur first closest to the word and so on. This is compared with a similar scattergram based on the words *Mauer/Grenze* prepared by the German assistant or a visitor from Germany. Further insights may be gained by providing information from a monolingual dictionary (*Sichtwechsel* [9]: 34–35 / *Typisch deutsch?* [6]: 136–139)

A variation on this is 'Word chase' (*Cultural awareness* [5]: 35)

9. Categorising

Students are given a jumble of words/phrases and have to divide them into a number of separate categories. This can help students to establish in their minds associations in the target language.

(*Typisch deutsch?* [6]: 137 and *Das sind wir* [10]: 21)

Recombine points of view

10. Comparing East and West German perspectives

(a) Written stimulus

Katrin Drechsel in her article '*So sehen wir das! Schülertexte aus Ost und West*' (*Fremdsprache Deutsch* 6), shows how personal responses of young people living in East and West Germany to the fall of the Berlin Wall can be used to highlight different perspectives. Students work in groups. They first have to read through the text they have been given and identify where the young person concerned comes from, presenting evidence from the text for their view. Next they are asked to identify key themes raised in the accounts and to present these to the whole class. This leads on to students considering how such themes feature within their own culture, thus adding a further perspective upon which to base comparisons. Finally the students are asked to compose a letter to one of the young people whose account they have read in which they ask questions, give their reactions, express their opinions and state their own position.

The texts presented in the article are drawn from a book by Helga Möricke, *Wir sind verschieden. Lebensentwürfe von Schülern aus Ost und West'.* [7] Another useful text for highlighting the mixed reaction of young people to re-unification is 'Der erste Eindruck — Schüler einer Klasse sehen zum ersten Mal Westberlin' taken from *Ich weiß nicht ob ich froh sein soll. Kinder erleben die Wende.* [8]

A selection of texts showing how re-unification affected the lives of ordinary people, from East and from West is presented in *Wende '89.*

(b) Spoken stimulus

The file of listening materials from Inter Nationes entitled *Von Aachen bis Zwickau* [11] contains interviews with young people from West Germany and the former DDR. Activities highlight the different perspectives from which issues are viewed depending on personal background and experience and reflect both short and longer term views. They demonstrate very effectively both the rational and the emotional elements in the way people respond to events. In one activity students hear seven young people stating what occurs to them when they think of German re-unification. The students complete a grid which lists the range of items mentioned by the young people. The students are then asked, on the basis of the information they have entered on the grid, to decide which of them come from former East Germany. In another activity students are presented with a drawing of a pair of scales and, having listened to an interview with a young woman from the former DDR, are asked to fill in on either side of the scale what she sees to be the advantages and the disadvantages of re-unification.

11. Comparing past and present

(a) Students are presented with a set of photographs of, in this case, Leipzig, showing changes between 1989 and 1991. They have to describe what the changes are. (*Das sind wir* [10]: 6–7)

(b) In a Spiegel article (46/91), included in *Brüderlich mit Herz und Hand?* [12], four young people from former East Germany comment on life since re-unification. In two groups students can be asked to summarise what is seen as positive and what as negative as a basis for further discussion.

(c) Students are given two timetables of an East German school student to compare changes since re-unification. They then listen to a pupil from former East Germany describing the changes and complete a grid highlighting these changes. Finally students are asked to note under headings differences between the Leipzig school and their own one. (*Das sind wir*[10]: 17–22)

Carrying out research

12. School-based survey

Students are asked to design a questionnaire on German re-unification to examine the attitudes of (e.g) the German assistant, German teachers, people with German connections in the school, other teachers, other pupils towards German re-unification. Students carry out a survey (in German or English as appropriate), analyse results and make an interpretation of them.

13. Fieldwork projects in Germany

In the previous section an idea was put forward for a form of school-based fieldwork. The opportunities for this kind of research are much greater, however, during a period of residence in the foreign country. Michael Byram[2] stresses that this should not mean just vaguely looking round, collecting a few brochures and haphazardly scribbling the odd note. Residence, according to him should only be called fieldwork if it is . . . *so structured that learners acquire insight into the foreign culture through direct experience coupled with reflection — related to the tradition of 'participant-observation' in ethnography.* This presupposes students receiving some training in fieldwork techniques (e.g. observing, interviewing, note-taking, making audio or video recordings, etc) and an introduction to anthropological and ethnographic concepts. Byram refers to the teaching of anthropology in the International Baccalauréat as a possible model and shows how such work can be built upon at university level to prepare students for longer stays abroad. Where stays abroad are combined with cross-curricular projects (as the EU is currently trying to encourage through the Socrates programme) which can involve link-ups via e-mail the possibilities for developing this kind of fieldwork are greatly increased.

In relation to German re-unification such a project could explore, for example, how life in a town in the former East Germany has changed since re-unification.

Forming and expressing opinions

14. Interpreting statistics

(a) On the basis of statistical information, e.g. the number of immigrants in Germany compared with Britain, students can be asked to prepare verbal summaries. This can inform discussion on the reasons for racist attacks in Germany and Britain in recent years. (*Brüderlich mit Hand und Herz*[12]: 47)

15. Agree or disagree?

Students are given a set of provocative statements (e.g. *In den neuen Bundesländern ist alles besser seit der Wende*). In groups they discuss whether they agree or disagree with the statement. If there is any disagreement in the group, the wording has to be changed so that everyone is happy with it. Each group reports on one or two statements before other groups are asked for alternative versions. (*Cultural awareness*[5]: 122–123)

16. Predicting

This is a technique which works especially well with video. After showing part of a recording the teacher pauses the tape and asks the students to predict what will happen next or what a particular person will say next (e.g. in response to a question). The next section of the video is then played after which the class discusses the degree to which what actually happened corresponded to their expectations. The activity is both a very good way to practise tenses and to raise awareness about the way we form judgements about others and about the danger of generalisation. One video programme with which this technique could be used is called *Die Wende* from the series *Jung in Deutschland*.[13] The programme profiles Lars, the son of a priest in former East Germany and shows what re-unification has meant to him.

17. Just a (cultural) minute

The rules are basically the same as those of the radio programme. The class is divided into teams. One person at a time has to talk on a particular topic for one minute. If the person hesitates or gives inaccurate information he or she can be challenged and it passes over to another team to continue and try to complete the minute. (*Cultural awareness*[5]: 148–149)

Interpreting and creating!

18. Taking the emotional temperature

(a) History through cartoons

The 1991 *Die Zeit* cartoon, 'Zur Gefühlslage der Nation' (see p68), paints a very clear picture of emotional disunity. The cartoon could be used as a springboard for discussion about what re-unification has meant at an emotional level for people living in the two parts of Germany and the reasons for this.

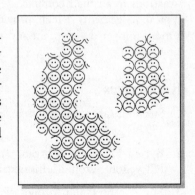

(b) History through song

The song *Marie* by the Leipzig group 'Karussell' expresses powerfully the euphoric feelings of Germans when the wall came down, but also the fact that it may take some time to achieve true unity.

19. Film reviews

Two recent German films which deal with re-unification are:

(a) *Stilles Land*, 1992, directed by Andreas Dresen which is centred on a provincial theatre company in the former DDR in the weeks leading up to the fall of the Berlin wall.

(b) *Das Versprechen*, 1994, directed by Margarethe von Trotta which is the story of two lovers who due to the division of Germany are only able to see each other four times in 28 years. This film also leads up to the opening of the wall.

Students could prepare a piece of writing (possibly as coursework) in the form of a review of one of these films or possibly comparing the two.

20. Interpretation and discussion of literary texts

- Wolf Biermann, *Ich halt's gut aus*
- Volker Braun, *Das Eigentum*
- Adel Karasholi, *Das Seil'*

Conclusion

'Aiming high' at 'A' level cannot be about treating language and culture as separate entities nor about trying to brush culture under the carpet. Underlying successful development as a student of language is a corresponding development in understanding and relating to different cultural experience. It is this ability to accept and come to terms with 'otherness', to see situations in all their complexity, to resist the temptation to accept stereotypical judgements which provides the foundation for developing both a more informed viewpoint and a more sensitive and discriminating use of language.

References

1 Stern H, *Issues and options in language teaching* (Oxford University Press, 1992)

2 Byram M and C Morgan, *Teaching and learning language and culture* (Clevedon, Avon: Multilingual Matters, 1994)

3 Hutchinson P and A Jones, *Wende '89 — Von der DDR zu den fünf neuen Ländern* (Bristol Classical Press, 1992)

4 Schmid G, *Kleine Deutschlandkunde. Ein erkundlicher Überblick* (Stuttgart: Ernst Klett Schulbuchverlag, 1994)

5 Tomalin B and S Stempleski, *Cultural awareness* (Oxford University Press, 1994)

6 Behal-Thomsen H, A Lundquist-Mog and P Mog, *Typisch deutsch? Arbeitsbuch zu Aspekten deutscher Mentalität* (Berlin: Langenscheidt, 1993)

7 Möricke H, *Wir sind verschieden. Lebensentwürfe von Schülern aus Ost und West* (Frankfurt: Luchterhand, 1991)

8 *Ich weiß nicht ob ich froh sein soll. Kinder erleben die Wende* (Metzler Verlag, 1990)

9 Hog M, B-D Muller, G Wessling and A Jones, *Sichtwechsel — Developing language sensitivity* (Cambridge University Press, 1989)

10 Meijer D, M von Kampenhout, E Weiß and J Schweckendiek, *Das sind wir — Leipziger Schüler berichten* (Goethe-Institut München, 1991)

11 Happe M and R Schmidt, *Von Aachen bis Zwickau — Jugendliche vor dem Mikro* (Bonn: Inter Nationes, 1994)

12 Schwager Y and J Kapuste, *Brüderlich mit Herz und Hand?* (Goethe-Institut London, 1992)

13 *Video profiles: Jung in Deutschland* (Cambridge University Press, 1993)

Chapter 6

'A' level teachers: are you tackling national stereotypes or ignoring them?

Salvador Estébanez

This chapter suggests that national stereotypes, if brought to the surface and challenged — rather than being supressed and hidden under the mantle of political correctness — can provide an initial motivational impetus in the language class, thus facilitating and encouraging cultural and linguistic understanding.

A varied selection of up-to-date press extracts is provided as well as exemplar material of how to exploit it in the classroom.

Introduction

The theme of the conference on which this book is based was focused on the need of 'A' level students to:

. . . develop their ability to analyse, to debate, to see the world from a wider perspective, to make and express critical judgements . . .

I believe that studying a foreign language should be a passage to a new vision of the world. Languages are identified with countries; countries have nationalities. National stereotypes are a caricature of the new vision that learning a foreign language should bring. As language teachers we tend to discourage jokes and stereotypical comments about nationalities, but we rarely attempt to turn them to our advantage.

Yet we cannot overestimate their influence. National stereotypes are very powerful because:

- they reflect the need of our mind to make generalisations in order to acquire knowledge; we look for patterns that can predict behaviour;
- national stereotypes do have some degree of truth in them. There is a widely held belief that there is such a thing as a nationality;
- they represent the **them** versus the **us**, which always was a powerful instinct necessary for survival.

We, as teachers, can fruitfully direct their motivational power. By identifying, analysing, debating, and laughing at them, we can provide depth to the superficial, complexity to the simplistic, we can attempt to move from the **us** to the **them** point of view. Then and only then, can we really choose our preferred vision of the world.

The suggested **didactic sequence** is as follows:

Step 1 Identify a present burning issue between the two countries concerned, e.g. 'fishing' between the UK and Spain.

Step 2 Collect examples of media coverage in the two countries, one in English, the other in Spanish.

Step 3 Analyse the content, identify the points of view and extract, if present, any use of Spanish stereotypes.

Step 4 Challenge the stereotypes:
- explore their origins (History and Geography)
- see the native's perspective: Literature, TV, Cinema, Painting, etc
- question real Spanish students

Step 5 Reflect on the English stereotypes.

Step 6 Design communicative activities based on the previous work.

Step 7 Analyse the language itself as a source of stereotyping.

Exemplar materials for these seven steps are provided. These suggestions and activities are possible ways of enabling our students to understand another cultural perspective. Although the need to use English has determined the choice of materials, it could easily have been done in another language.

Steps 1, 2 & 3   Spanish and British media coverage of 'fishing'

THE ARMADA — SPAIN — BULLFIGHTING

The Sunday Telegraph, 14 August 1994

Forget Torremolinos and flamenco; the key to the Spaniard is fish. His name for tuna is *atún* (specialising as he does in anagrams, such as Otan, for Nato). De Gaulle's little joke was that the French are ungovernable with their 246 kinds of cheese. The Spaniard is ungovernable and a lover of even more kinds of fish. The Spaniard gets all the cash he can from the EC, but his motive in the Tuna War is hunger for duels of honour, and for fish.

What is the Spaniard's future? Will he even exist? He speaks a different language from his compatriots: Franco tried to make him speak Castilian. Now he speaks Valencian or Catalan, Aragonese or Basque. At a town on the Portuguese border the roadsigns announcing 'Tuy' have been painted over by Galician nationalists to read 'Tui': it is pronounced exactly the same.

Angel Ganivet (1865–98) wrote: *Spain is an absurd country and metaphysically impossible; absurdity is its nerve and mainstay. Its turn to prudence will denote its end.* Perhaps prudence means socialism, the EC and regionalism. The Spaniard was ever a solipsist and his instincts are fissiparous: *Mas vale ser cabeza de raton que cola de leon* — better be the head of a mouse than the tail of a lion. Whoever wins the Tuna War, the Spaniard is an endangered species.

They're playing our tuna . . .

Newlyn's fishermen rely on tuna catches to survive. But they fear new clashes with the Spanish fleet as the season begins.

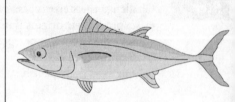

La mar para los peces . . . y para los 'ingleses'

El País, jueves 20 de abril de 1995

'Continúan siendo apresados en otras partes del mundo por sus malas prácticas de pesca', declaró Wells al diario *The Globe and Mail.* 'Todo el mundo debiera saber lo irresponsables que son las prácticas de pesca españolas, y si los europeos no pueden pararles, Canadá tendrá que hacerlo', agregó.

La legislación canadiense de 1994 y sus medidas de aplicación a barcos españoles y portugueses en 1995 suponen una planificada política de fuerza — incluido el uso de las armas — que podrá ser jaleada por los *hooligans* — aqui el inglés es obligado — de la mar, pero es bochornosa y, sobre todo,

absolutamente illegal en sus principios y en sus métodos. La demanda planteada por España captura y produce del orden de 1.400.000 toneladas de productos pesqueros e importa otras 600.000 para atender a la demanda de su población.

CAMBIO16, 8 Agosto 1994, No 1.185

Las diferentes artes de pesca empleadas por franceses y españoles son la principal causa de los conflictos en la temporada del atún. Mientras en España los sistemas más comunes son el currican o cacea, el cebo vivo y la palangre, en Francia utilizan las redes de deriva o volantas y las de arrastre. Las diferencias fundamentales entre ellos radica principalmente en que al usar los métodos españoles se obtiene pescado de mayor calidad; se produce un menor perjuicio ecológico y tiene el 'inconveniente' de que se recoge menor cantidad de ejemplares.

'Hay demasiados pescadores para pocos peces'

LAS MALVINAS

DRAKE – NELSON – INGLATERRA – GIBRALTAR

Step 4 — Challenging stereotypes

A student may say:

Spanish people are lazy; they do things so slowly . . . it is always mañana . . . they even have a siesta in the afternoon!

The teacher may use this utterance as a challenge which needs to be met. This dialogue between students and teachers may lead to some interesting project work:

Student: Why do Spaniards eat so much at lunch time?

Teacher: Because they have a long break before going back to work; they may even go to have a siesta!

Student: Why do they have such a long break at lunch time?

Teacher: Because it is very hot to do anything else!

Student: Why don't they have air-conditioning?

Teacher: They do, but the break is an old habit. It goes back to when the majority of workers were peasants and it was too hot to work in the fields. They would get up very early in the morning, go to work and come back home at lunch time. They returned to the fields in the evening.

Student: But only a small minority work now in agriculture . . .

Teacher: Yes, but that is only true recently. Spain, unlike Britain, did not have a real industrial revolution until the sixties. Thus, the changes are very recent.

Student: But, for example, how can a shop assistant have a proper life if he works from 9 to 2 and then from 5 to 8?

Teacher: Well, it is hard for modern workers. Many of them are moving to European timetables, particularly schools and factories. Why don't we find what the present position is by designing a questionnaire and asking our language assistant and our penfriends in Spain?

Looking at literature

All literary works are wonderful sources for tackling national stereotypes. There are very few modern and contemporary Spanish writers who do not attempt to identify the Spanish national characteristics. Ganivet and Madariaga use the psychological route; Américo Castro and Menéndez Pidal via History; Unamuno and Ortega via Philosophy; Díaz-Plaja and Carandell via humour; Machado and Cela follow the literary road . . .

| Step 5 | English stereotypes |

We need authentic materials for our courses, particularly newspapers. The English press is a rich source for this theme.

1 'The English are very traditional'

Beppe Severgnini: *The Economist* (8/1/94): 'An Italian in London'

Any sensible Italian envies the British love and respect for tradition. The trouble is that very often the British love of what is ancient and well-known turns into fear of what is new and unknown . . . Even John Major's 'back to basics' theme sounds ominously reassuring.

2 'The English are very polite'

James Morgan, *Financial Times:* 'As they say in Europe' (Correspondent of the BBC World Service)

The delicacy of the British struck me in a bus which had a sign saying, 'We would prefer you not to eat or drink on this bus. However, if you do would you please take your litter with you.' I spent some time working out how this would translate. German is not suitable for conveying moral uncertainty or the doctrine of the second best. In French the warning is like something from a home for the incontinent elderly; in Italian, an invitation to steal the bus; in Czech, the sign would be a trap to ensnare the man with a sandwich in an endless bureaucratic nightmare.

3 'The English dislike intellectuals'.

The Evening Standard on the editorial 'Clever William' of 15 June 1995:

The Prince of Wale's twelve-year-old son, Prince William, has passed his Common Entrance examination and will board at Eton College from the autumn, the first heir to our throne who has ever done so. The prince is said to be a clever boy. So might we one day be ruled by an intellectual monarch? Prince Charles's ventures into intellectuallism — not to mention his father Prince Philip's safaris into the world of ideas — have often attracted odious comment. Both went to Gordonstoun. If William turns out to be very clever, perhaps his Eton mentors will bequeath to him one of the ancient school's greatest gifts: the ability to conceal it.

Auberon Waugh in the *Daily Telegraph*, 28 June 1995:

Redwood's fatal flaw is that he obviously thinks he is clever. Really clever people in England spend most of their time pretending to be stupid. The English dislike and mistrust clever people.

4 What about name calling?

Louis Palabrota, *Metromania:* Racism

Wop remains the favourite put-down for an Italian. It derives from the Sicilian and Neopolitan greeting Guappol — 'Hi, handsome.' This greeting, common in Spain, may date from the 14th century, when Sicily was ruled from Barcelona. Sicilian children are to this day admonished with 'Behave, or I'll call the Catalans.' The Spanish call Catalan polacos (Poles), heaven knows why.

| Step 6 | Linguistic exploitation (1) |

Laughing at stereotypes: the Mills & Boon Nationality Test

Instructions: for those unfamiliar with the genre, Mills and Boon is romantic fiction with reliable 100 per cent stereotyped characters. The test presents five such characters and the students have to guess their EU nationality. Read the description of the following five characters (underlined) and try to guess their nationality. They belong to either France, Spain, Germany, Italy or the UK.

Do not try to answer until you have read all the descriptions.

1 The girl melted as <u>he</u> expertly held her in his arms and kissed her lips.

2 <u>He</u> stood impassive, his eyes mere slits, as she slapped him, 'You're a cold fish — you lied all along!'

3 <u>She</u> stood at the foot of the stairs, eyes flashing, quivering with emotion, 'If you dance with another woman, I'll kill you', she spat out.

4 The girl sighed, 'Oh you are so wonderful!'. <u>He</u> stood there acknowledging the truth of the statement with a superior little smile.

5 'Please, don't leave me' She screamed. But the <u>man</u> stood, arrogant, nostrils flaring, 'You have defiled my family name, it's over!'

ANSWERS: 1 _____   2 _____

3 _____   4 _____

5 _____

Solution: 1 French, 2 German, 3 Italian, 4 English, 5 Spanish

| Step 6 | Linguistic exploitation (2) |

Laughing at stereotypes: an enforced prejudice technique

Write at least five positive and five negative adjectives for each nationality.

Here are a selection of adjectives that you may use:

> *proud, formal, polite, rough, intolerant, cruel, passionate, reliable, faithful, haughty, honourable, truthful, modest, arrogant, smug, self-effacing . . .*

Please add any of your own.

POSITIVO		NEGATIVO	
SPANISH	ENGLISH	SPANISH	ENGLISH

'One World in Europe' CILT January/Enero 1993 at City University, London

POSITIVO		NEGATIVO	
SPANISH	ENGLISH	SPANISH	ENGLISH
proud	conscientious	cruel	smug
passionate	reliable	intolerant	arrogant
formal	reserved	arrogant	self-effacing
honourable	self-effacing	unreliable	formal
festive	orderly	lazy	proud
colourful	modest	haughty	insensitive
relaxed	faithful	disorganised	cold
musical	polite	hypocondriac	self-conscious
direct	truthful		
reckless			

Dyffring Conference, February 1993

POSITIVO		NEGATIVO	
SPANISH	**ENGLISH**	**SPANISH**	**ENGLISH**
passionate	polite	intolerant	smug
dignified	formal	lazy	arrogant
relaxed	reliable	superstitious	cold
honourable	self-effacing	arrogant	shy
polite	reasonable	cruel	intolerant
friendly	precise	unpunctual	self-satisfied
flamboyant	modest	noisy	narrow-minded
musical	ironic	sexist	snobbish
	organised	disorganised	rough
		unreliable	boorish

Aiming high 'A' level Cilt Conference, July 1995

POSITIVO		NEGATIVO	
SPANISH	**ENGLISH**	**SPANISH**	**ENGLISH**
passionate	polite	cruel	smug
proud	reliable	arrogant	haughty
honourable	modest	proud	intolerant
warm	formal	rough	arrogant
generous		haughty	cold

Is not the level of agreement shown by all participants (on three separate occasions) frightening, considering that it is an open-ended test?

Step 6	Linguistic exploitation (3)

Common English-Spanish Stereotypes

1   Match the four following sets to the four categories:

(1) keep their word.

(2) cold stodgy food and luke-warm beer.

(3) cheerful, good food, a place to retire, most attactive men and women.

(4) have not preserved real quality of life, are not preserving the environment.

POSITIVO		NEGATIVO	
SPANISH	**ENGLISH**	**SPANISH**	**ENGLISH**

2 Fill in the gaps with either the word **Spanish** or **English**:

a The _____(1) are not fanatical clock followers; but they seem in a hurry when they are in a queue. The _____(2) follow the clock and the queue, and they also say 'sorry' as they push you out of the way.

b The _____(3) are not comfortable talking about the body; the _____(4) are more comfortable, even keen. The _____(5) may tell you all that is wrong with their bodies, the _____(6) talk about illnesses with an eye for detail.

c If the _____(7) feel alarmed about talking about the body, they feel terrified about touching it. Although the _____(8) had once a reputation for kissing, now the _____(9) are at a loss even when they meet their own family. The _____(10) are quite happy to embrace, to put their arms around your back, to touch you to add emotion to their words.

d The _____(11) instinctively dislike language which is pompous and condescending; the _____(12) seem to sound both quite effortlessly!

e The _____(13) are good at being formal, they can be informal but they are very aware of the suitable register for the occasion. The _____(14) are good at being informal, they can be formal but they often go over the top.

f The _____(15) are dreamers walking in the clouds, the _____(16) are shopowners walking in the pavement.

g The _____(17) think that the Catholic Church is to do with religion; the _____(18) think that the Church of England is something between a cricket club and a choir.

h The _____(19) think that the family includes at least grandparents and children; the _____(20) think that the family is an exercise in reproduction which can last a maximum of eighteen years.

i The _____(21) are snobs when it comes to language, the _____(22) are snobs about clothes. A _____(23) working-class family would be horrified about buying second-hand clothes.

j The _____(24) love hyperbole, imagination, improvisation and passion. The _____(25) love understatement, precision, planning and moderation.

Solution Spanish: 1, 4, 5, 6, 10, 12, 14, 15, 17, 19, 22, 23, 24
English: 2, 3, 7, 8, 9, 11, 13, 16, 18, 20, 21, 25

| Step 6 | Linguistic exploitation (4) |

Nacionalidades de España

Coloca en el cuadro los 5 grupos de 5 adjetivos cada uno con la región/nacionalidad que mejor crees que encaja:

A	B	C
1 nobles	1 fuertes	1 graciosos
2 orgullosos	2 separatistas	2 exagerados
3 honrados	3 comilones	3 juerguistas
4 religiosos	4 extremistas	4 charlatanes
5 sencillos	5 trabajadores	5 abiertos

D	E
1 prácticos	1 cariñosos
2 responsables	2 amantes de su tierra
3 emprendedores	3 supersticiosos
4 ambiciosos	4 hogareños
5 tacaños	5 sufridos

ANDALUCES	CASTELLANOS	CATALANES
1 _____	1 _____	1 _____
2 _____	2 _____	2 _____
3 _____	3 _____	3 _____
4 _____	4 _____	4 _____
5 _____	5 _____	5 _____

GALLEGOS	VASCOS
1 _____	1 _____
2 _____	2 _____
3 _____	3 _____
4 _____	4 _____
5 _____	5 _____

Solution: A = Castellanos B = Vascos C = Andaluces D = Gallegos E = Catalanes

| Step 7 | The role of language itself in stereotypes |

A few anecdotes based on real experiences provide evidence that as the role of language in human behaviour increases, it is far more difficult to be objective in assessing attitudes. In the first anecdote there is no verbal exchange, therefore the situation can be assessed 'naked' without the verbal dressing.

First anecdote

A group of 30 English teachers of Spanish were doing an enhancement language course in the University of Navarra. As part of the course I took them for a day trip to the Pyrenees. When we got to the village of Roncal, the birthplace of the Spanish composer and violinist Sarasate, we visited his memorial and then we visited the local trout farm.

A worker was feeding the fish and we gathered around him. The worker, **wanting to entertain us**, picked up a trout and threw it on a net, outside the water, for us to enjoy seeing the beautiful fish. At first everybody enjoyed the spectacle: the wonderful fish jumping acrobatically on the net trying to get back to the water. Then, a second later, the English teachers' faces showed concern. Finally they showed horror. I realised it was a disaster but I could not make the worker understand that he had to put the trout immediately back in the water. After a few seconds it was safely back among trout colleagues. I still thanked the Spanish worker for his efforts to please us.

When we re-started our journey I thought I would explain that the trout farm was part of a government scheme to try to fill the rivers again with new trout. A teacher and friend told me *Salvador, don't say anything...* I did not say anything but I remembered the article by Libby Purves in the *Times*, 28 June 1995:

There is a bitter, eternal irony in the way that poor Vicky Moore, the animal campaigner, was gored and tossed and all but killed by a Spanish bull. Ms Moore is famously the most hated woman in Spain; ever since her epic rescue of Blackie the Donkey, so threatened does she feel by the nation of bullfighters that she was travelling under a false name and in disguise. But it was the bull that got her, not the picadors.

However, my silence was no good, the ghost of Spanish cruelty to animals — bulls, donkeys . . . — had been re-awakened in the teachers' minds. However, a few hour later we all happily ate *trout a la navarra* — cooked with cured ham — without as much as a second thought.

Not having verbal exchanges helps to evaluate the attitudes of the worker and the teachers. The English and the trout agreed that the Spanish worker was insensitive because it was an unnecessary suffering. The fact that the worker wanted to entertain the teachers was not counted as an attenuating factor. Later, at lunch time, the English and the trout disagreed about the pleasure of the latter being eaten by the former.

Second anecdote

John went to Spain to spend two weeks with his friend Pablo. The first three mornings John said, *¡Buenos días!* as he entered in the kitchen, Pablo answered *¡Buenos días!* the first two, but the third time he said *Do you know what we are going to do today?* This unexpected response made John slightly worried, he thought he might have done something wrong. Later, however, John became accustomed to the inconsistency of Spanish greetings among close relatives or friends in familiar contexts. Towards the end of the two weeks, John automatically replied to Pablo's *¡Hola!* and continued watching TV. Pablo got worried, he thought that John was cross. Later, however, he realised, that to an English person, a greeting is just a greeting: when one is greeted *How are you?* the last thing one does is to try to really respond.

Even at this basic verbal exchange, there is room for misinterpretation: Spanish greeting inconsistency worried John; the formality of English greetings worried Pablo. Fortunately, they had enough time to find out they were worrying unnecesarily.

Third anecdote

A few weeks ago a Director of Education from southern Spain came to a home county in England to sign an agreement of cooperation between both education departments. After all the formalities of the signing ceremony, the two parties established a very friendly and informal relationship. Later on we all went to dinner and had a marvellous time until the Spanish Director looked at the waiter and asked *Bread!* The waiter, with a disapproving face thinking that foreigners were difficult, went to fetch it; the English felt a criticism had been made. The Spaniard never realised what was going on. Over an hour later, the time came to choose the dessert. The English Director asked his Spanish colleague if he wanted some dessert. I translated. The Spanish Director said: *poooostre . . . nooooooo/dessert . . . no*

I did not need to translate. The English party, particularly embarrassed by the presence of the waiter, thought that the Spanish director was being rude and/or that something must have gone wrong.

Yet the interpretation of the message had all been wrong; what the Spanish Director was trying to communicate was:

> *I had such a superb meal that I am afraid I could not possibly contemplate having a dessert as well*

I knew it because he had told me so in no uncertain Spanish terms. However, the English heard *nooooo . . .* but they did not understand the **Spanish intonation** which was carrying the true message.

It is then possible to begin to misinterpret even at this very prosodic level. A *nooooo*, which appears so unequivocal, is easily misinterpreted.

Fourth anecdote

> *I play a little golf* said John.
> *I play good golf* said Antonio.

John listening to Antonio thought *What a boastful beast!*

Antonio, having been thoroughly beaten by John, thought *What a hypocrite!*

The English language has **understatement** as its main attitudinal foundation. In this anecdote we can see that language is not very objective in assessing golf levels. We have now an Englishman and a Spaniard thinking of each other as a boaster and a hypocrite; but are they really so?

The English and Spanish languages

Trying to identify the defining characteristics of a social group is part of Sociology. Linguistics look at the characteristics of a language. However, even the linguistic nature of the language itself gives rise to stereotypes.

Spaniards speaking English think that English people do not make a proper effort to understand them. They think that they pronounce allrrrright, but the English say, *sorry?*

> Juan: *Pass peas please!*
> David: *Sorry? What is he talking about?*

Juan thinks that he speaks very clearly but in fact his peas could be peace, or even piece.

There are twelve vowel phonemes in English and five in Spanish; English words are shorter; therefore it is very easy for an English person to misunderstand — understand another word which is phonetically very close — rather than not understand. It is more difficult to reestablish communication from a misunderstanding than from non-understanding.

So, are Spaniards right when they think that the English do not make an effort to understand?

English people think that the Spaniards speak very fast: za pa za pa za pa . . . in spite of the lisp!

Spanish is a syllabic language. All the syllables are clearly pronounced. For example, the word 'secretary' is pronounced 'se-cre-ta-ria' whereas in English is SEcretary. So a word which is similar in written form becomes four units of sound in Spanish versus two in English. No surprise that the English think that Spaniards speak Spanish like machine guns. No surprise either that the Spaniards think that the English can not pronounce their own language properly!

Conclusion

Is the notion of the proud Spaniard dependent upon the ubiquity of flaring nostrils among Spaniards, or is it that the Spanish language itself, when translated, sounds to an English ear, full of pride and pomposity?

The anecdotes show the dangers of passing judgement when linguistic elements are involved. Linguistic awareness, as well as cultural, is a precondition for objective assessment.

Finally, I would advise teachers to draw their students' attention to the difference between aesthetic and ethical statements. We are all entitled to express our aesthetic preferences, but we must be aware of the dangers of passing ethical judgements. A Spaniard saying that English is a difficult language to learn is fine, a Spaniard saying that English people do not make an effort to understand foreigners is untrue.

Further reading

Amodia J, 'Un español frente al espejo' in *Vida Hispánica,* no 11 (ALL, June 1995)

'A'

Part four

•

The challenge of literature

Chapter 7

Working with German literary texts

Susan Tebbutt

As the millennium approaches, students are increasingly aware that the ability to speak another European language gives a competitive edge in the employment market, especially since the borders within Europe have opened up. The profile of the average student of 'A' level German today is radically different to that of twenty years ago, when the combination of German, French and English Literature was common. Today few students choose only Arts subjects at 'A' level, and even fewer would list the chance to study German literature as a key motivating factor for choosing German as an 'A' level subject. Since many students are not avid readers in their mother tongue, and perceive the study of literature as a daunting prospect, it might appear that there was a case for avoiding the study of literature if given the option. I would like to argue, however, that the broad field of German literature offers a wide range of intellectual challenges, with something to appeal to all students.

Moving from GCSE reading texts to 'A' level literary texts: developing reading competence

Students beginning their 'A' level German have limited experience of reading German. The GCSE syllabus is anchored firmly within the parameters of functional transactions and the language of everyday life, and although syllabi stress the importance of wide reading, in practice, there is a race against the clock to cover the wide range of topics in the time available, because of the time constraints under which the great majority of British foreign language learners suffer. Whereas German students may have started the English language at the age of ten and cope with progressively longer sections of text, the average British student will not have read more than a few pages of German at the start of the 'A' level course.[1] The shortfall is made even clearer if it is appreciated that the average ten-year-old German has heard and spoken German for some 36,500 hours (ten years of at least ten hours a day) whereas the average British student starting an 'A' level German course has only had a maximum of 300 hours of class contact time (three years, starting in Y9, with some 120 weeks with 2.5 hours of class contact per week). The end result is that the English student has had a thousandth of the time that the native speaker has had listening to and speaking the language.

Testing reading skills

GCSE Higher Reading	'A' level Literature Paper
short extracts from authentic texts	works of 50–200 pages
understanding of meaning of vocabulary items and listing of points made	evaluation of writer's intentions and analysis of impact of words
scrutiny of individual characters and themes	comparison of several characters and themes

In order to succeed at the GCSE Higher Reading Exam,[2] students need to be able to follow at most a page of authentic written German. The minimum length for an 'A' level text, however, is approximately fifty pages and the majority of prescribed texts are between 100 and 200 pages in length.

Question 9 of the 1995 NEAB Higher Reading exam (see Appendix A) contains the longest piece of consecutive prose to be found in that exam paper. The question is typical in that it checks the ability to extract key vocabulary items, and does not necessarily require the student to understand the text from beginning to end. No questions are set, for example, on the last sentence of the first paragraph about life in Turkey.

Question 14(b) from the NEAB 1995 'A' level German literature paper (see Appendix B) seems at first glance to be also testing the ability to understand a relatively short passage, but the question makes it clear that the student is expected to be able to place the passage 'in its precise context'. In terms of the depth of analysis expected, the GCSE student is asked to make a straight-forward judgement on the attitude of Turkish men towards women, where-as in questions such as 14(c) the 'A' level student is expected to be able to compare and contrast a number of characters and themes.

How then can students make the leap from reading extracts of one page or less to understanding whole books? An extensive graded reading programme is essential.[3] It is, however, virtually impossible to find texts which follow on seamlessly from GCSE. There are few literary works which conveniently revolve round hotels, meals, trains and the weather, and the language of literature tends to be more abstract and far less predictable, with the range of verbs far, far wider than that previously encountered.

Some of the available series of short readers fulfil a bridging function, but tend to be dull and uninspiring. Since the 1980s there has been a steady increase in the number of works of *Jugendliteratur* studied by students of German as a foreign language, both in Britain and in other European countries, since the language tends to be contemporary and conversational and the plot straightforward. Works such as Gudrun Pausewang's collections of short stories *Es ist doch alles grün* (1991) and *Friedensgeschichten* (1985) and Peter Härtling's novel *Oma* (1975) may be tackled near the start of the 'A' level course. Works such as *Sind es noch die alten Farben?* (1987) [4] or *Sie haben mich zu einem Ausländer gemacht* (1984) [5] contain a mixture of shorter and longer texts, which allow the more able reader to be stretched, whilst motivating the weaker student. The *Themen und Texte* series of '*Didaktische Vorschläge zur Bearbeitung von themengebundenen Jugendbüchern*' edited by Elke Dehmel, published by the Goethe-Institut in Manchester, combine hints on motivating a group for work with the particular text, together with detailed suggestions for discussions, and classroom activities.

It would be wrong to suggest that 'A' level students cannot tackle works written for a general audience. Over the years a number of works such Heinrich Böll's short stories or Max Frisch' play *Biedermann und die Brandstifter* (1961) have become very popular texts for study during the first year of the 'A' level course. It is important to remember that although the teacher may have read these works dozens of time, they are fresh to each generation of German 'A' level students, and can be studied from a number of different theoretical angles, as will be explained later.

The four skills of listening, reading, speaking and writing cannot be taught in isolation from each other, and that students should be developing proficiency in understanding German by watching German TV and videos, listening to cassettes, working with computer software programmes, having regular conversation lessons with the German assistant and/or participating in a study visit or exchange programme to Germany. Students should aim to widen their active and passive vocabulary in order to acquire a *Sprachgefühl*. Today it is normal for the 'A' level course to be taught entirely in German, whereas twenty years ago many students generally discussed their 'A' level literature texts in English, wrote essays on them in English, and in some cases even read the text in English translation, and in this respect today's students are in a better position in terms of broad exposure to the German language.

Choosing a text

Having built up reading fluency by reading a number of shortish works, students are ready to study a work in more depth. Increasingly, students are being given the opportunity to set their own agenda for study, but most teachers will still wish to study at least one text with the group as a whole.

Selecting literary texts — key criteria:

length of work	complexity of language
interest of text to teacher	relevance of theme to students

Given that students have a limited experience of reading German, it is best to start with a relatively short work, but even very short works may be written in such complex language that students have difficulty progressing. The teacher should actually find the text interesting and stimulating, since it is otherwise difficult to convince students why the group is working on it. Given the non-homogeneous nature of German 'A' level groups, it is best to pick a work of general contemporary relevance, linked if possible to a special concern of the city or region where the students live (e.g. women's rights, the environment, conservation, labour migration, etc). Where possible, a film or theatre production of the work itself or another by the same author helps to give a work more immediate appeal.

What is German literature? Is it work by . . .

- dead writers
- male writers
- German writers
- writers of fiction
- documentary writers
- writers of biography, autobiography, travel literature

- contemporary writers
- female writers
- Austrian, German, Italian, Swiss, or Turkish writers
- writers of novels
- writers for adults
- writers for young people

German Literature is no longer synonymous with Goethe and Schiller. In the earlier part of the twentieth century there was a rigid literary canon, and university students worked their way through from Old High German texts to the Classical and Romantic period through to the present day. Generally it was felt that critics did not have sufficient distance from contemporary literature and that such works had not yet 'stood the test of time'. In the post-war period, debates have been opened up as to what constitutes literature, and the dominance of the study of male writers has been challenged. In today's multi-cultural society it is important to recognise the role played by *MigrantInnenliteratur*, as well as works by Austrian or Swiss writers. The term *Literatur* in German can refer to fiction or non-fiction, and documentary literature, such as Ayse und Devrim's *Wo gehören wir hin?* (1983)[6] offers students insights into German society.

Biographies, such Hermann Vinke's *Das kurze Leben der Sophie Scholl* (1980) or Mirjam Pressler's account of Anne Frank, *Ich sehne mich so* (1992) or autobiographies, such as Inge Auerbacher's *Ich bin ein Stern* (1986)[7] and travel literature such as the account by theologian Dorothea Sölle entitled *Gott im Müll: Eine andere Entdeckung Lateinamerikas* (1992) may not necessarily appeal to all members of a group, but may spark a life-long interest in a particular person or theme. Nowadays *Jugendliteratur* is as much the subject of academic research as adult literature,[8] and even students with an excellent command of the German language should not feel that such works are only to be studied by those less confident in their reading skills. Students tend to be more apprehensive about **how** to respond to works than about whether or not they can understand the language.

Methodological approaches to literature

Whereas there are many piano teachers who include elements of theory from the first lesson onwards, rather than suddenly introducing theory once the basics of playing have been mastered, it is rare to find teachers of literary texts who integrate a study of literary criticism into their teaching of literature.[9]

The majority of teachers feel that the first priority is that the text is understood, and that only then can aspects of theory or methodology be introduced, but I feel that an awareness of literary theory from the start can heighten enjoyment rather than diminish enthusiasm. In *A Reader's Guide to Contemporary Literary Theory* (1993) Selden and Widdowson argue that *far from having a sterile effect on our reading, new ways of seeing literature can revitalise our engagement with texts.*[10] The advantage of highlighting methodology is that the student becomes more aware that the skills learnt in studying a text may be transferable to the study of another text at a later stage. Although 'A' level questions appear on the surface to be far more accessible to a wider range of candidates than they were twenty years ago, and no longer always explicitly mention theoretical issues, there can be no doubt that candidates scoring the highest marks are those who have a deeper awareness of literary criticism which goes beyond the ability to recount and categorise aspects of plot and characterisation.

Many students claim to have a built-in suspicion of studying literature, but this is often precisely because they cannot understand the purpose of the study and worry that they will not be able to come up with an acceptable critique. This fear can be bypassed by laying down clear guidelines and stating learning targets **before** starting to read a work. It is not the case that studying literary theory will make this more difficult. On the contrary, students will have the sense of satisfaction that they are formulating their own individual responses to a text, rather than merely reading the secondary literature available and then condensing its findings in their essays.

How does literary theory relate to the type of tasks set in 'A' level literature exam papers?

Approaches to literature	
Approach	**Characteristics**
humanist	linked to writer's life and outlook
formalist	investigates text in isolation
Marxist	interprets literature in its social and historical context
structuralist	analyses codes used to construct meaning
feminist	focuses on gender issues
post-colonialist	focuses on ethnocentricity
reader-orientated	centred on reader's reactions

Up until the late 1960s almost all 'A' level literary questions were based on the humanist approach to literature, which revolves round knowledge of a writer's life, work and style. Many editions of set books include an introduction which outlines this information. This is the equivalent to the method of teaching history which involves providing students with dates and names, which have to be regurgitated later. Students do not necessarily have to form their own opinion, but may merely reproduce those of the 'experts'.

From the formalist school of literary criticism comes the 'context question', in which students are asked to comment on a section of text in isolation. Preparation for this type of question again tends to involve learning set responses and technical terms for features of literary style. Students often like the 'context question' since they can see the limits of the question more clearly, and can learn how to include relevant pieces of information.

The Marxist interpretation of literature as anchored in its political, social and historical context is paid indirect homage in the proliferation of questions which ask candidates what they learn about a particular period of history or social issue (e.g. First World War, Third Reich, unemployment, drug abuse, etc). Many teachers turn gratefully to this type of question, since they feel that their students will be interested in the social/historical/political issue and will thus be motivated to read the work. Texts like the *Stern* reporters' account of a teenage drug-addict, *Christiane F* (1990), Heinrich Böll's *Die verlorene Ehre der Katharina Blum* (1974) and Günter Wallraff's *Ganz Unten* (1985) have been extremely popular with students, especially since films have been made based on the works. There is, however, a need to remind students that a literary work does **not** provide direct sociological or historical evidence, and they should also focus on representation of the issues, rather than merely assembling a balance-sheet of social/political/ historical points for the examiner.

The structuralist approach to literature may involve analysing the implicit and explicit ideology of a text, by examining the codes and language used. In any given year there are, nation-wide, a small proportion of bilingual students or native speakers of German, and such students may find the structuralist approach particularly challenging and rewarding.

The last twenty years have seen the flourishing of feminist and post-colonialist theories of literary criticism, and both can lead to some very stimulating work on the part of students. There is today a far higher general level of awareness of gender and race issues, and it is important in multi-cultural Britain to emphasise to students that the German-speaking world is also a multi-ethnic community. Since less work has been done in this field than, say, in the area of humanist research into literature, students have more opportunity to follow channels of investigation which have not already been over-researched. There also many openings here for original comparative pieces of research.

The final type of literary theory is reader-orientated research. At university level this might take the form of questionnaires and surveys into the reception of a work over a geographical area or a particular period in time. Obviously 'A' level students would not have time to undertake such extensive research, but may be asked to produce a highly personal response to a text. This may take the form of an extract from an imaginary diary, a newspaper article, or an imaginary television or radio show with interviews with characters from the work. There is tremendous scope for lateral thinking and innovative approaches here, but in practice, some students may see this type of exercise as an easy option, and produce a piece of work which is little more than a glorified *Nacherzählung*. It is crucial that students arrange facts and information and reactions in order to create a new work, which should not be derivative or open to the charge of plagiarism, but should show signs of intertextuality — references to the original text — which render the new creation comprehensible. The empathetic approach can produce high levels of motivation at group and individual level.

Preparing texts

Preparing a piece of German literary text poses additional problems to the preparation of a text written in the student's mother tongue. It is essential that the student should both follow the intricacies of plot and characterisation and also be aware of the register and linguistic features of the text. It is important to introduce as many tasks as possible involving active use of key vocabulary. Factual questions on the text are necessary, but students should also be encouraged from the start to analyse as well as recount, even if their first utterances are of the very simple *Ich finde es interessant, weil . . .* type. When they are preparing the text students are building a portfolio of material in German which they can refer to later, and should be learning from their mistakes. Students may be given a jumbled set of sentences which summarise a chapter or section of a work and asked to rearrange them in the correct order, or be given sentences split in two which they have to re-assemble. These exercises involve writing in German but do not involve constructing sentences from scratch. Once students are more proficient they should be able to take turns to provide the jumbled summary or sentences.

At the preparatory stage it is important that students discuss as many aspects of a work as possible, including their own reactions and comparisons with other works if relevant. Enacting scenes from a work will help students empathise with characters and enable them to try out their ideas on others. It is important that students write up some of these tasks, so that they receive constructive feedback on their use of language and understanding of the text. The production of a fictional diary is an excellent preparatory exercise, since the student is using the language related to the theme of the text and is making decisions about the relative significance of different events and characters.

Students may look specifically for strengths and weaknesses, may concentrate on evidence of characterisation or may be looking out for examples of prejudice or bias in a text. The use of contrasts may help students formulate responses. If working on the theme of war, for example, it may well prove fruitful to look at a work on the theme of peace, since the differences stand out clearly. If studying the image of Turkish girls in a work written by a German, it may help to look at a text about the same theme written by a Turkish writer.

Structuring and redrafting essays on literary themes

When students prepare a literary essay, it is helpful if they are given guidelines right from the start as to how to lay out their essay and bibliography. Rather than just picking up a pen and writing, students should present a plan to the teacher first. Terms and framework of reference should be defined and then the main part of the essay will probably fall into three or four sections, followed by a conclusion, which should not introduce new evidence. It may help to decide roughly on the balance of the essay in terms of numbers of words, since otherwise there is a tendency to write at length on the first point and then skimp on the second or third, when it becomes clear that the word limit is fast approaching.

Developing competence in writing essays on literary themes

brainstorm → plan work → select quotations and evidence
→ write an introduction → develop ideas and reach
a conclusion → review and redraft work

If a group is working together on a project it helps to start by brainstorming. Students note down all the ideas then work in pairs to order the ideas, discarding some points at this stage if necessary. Students then need to decide which ideas are the most important and put them in a logical sequence. Before writing the essay, students should go through their notes and the text they are studying and note down any quotations they wish to use and points they wish to make. The quotations and points should then be allocated to the different sections of the essay. It is helpful to take a clean sheet of paper for each sub-section of the essay and list the ideas, one per line, one underneath the other, rather than in continuous prose form, so that arrows or lines can be drawn linking particular ideas or quotations.

The writing of the essay itself is easier if the student thinks of two or three key words or phrases for each sub-section of the essay. The introduction should explain what the essay is about and what the writer is trying to demonstrate. In the case of a narrative piece it is equally important that the essay is well-structured, although the structure may be less immediately apparent to the reader.

In the main body of the essay the student should develop ideas, either in a 'first, second and third' format or in a 'these are the advantages' and 'these are the disadvantages' or 'these are the positive aspects of . . .' and 'these are the negative aspects of . . .' format, and then round off the essay with a conclusion.

The final stage, which is far easier if students are word processing their work, is that they should leave their work for at least a day and then review it. They should re-read it to see whether it makes sense, whether the points are made unambiguously and whether the quotations illustrate points being made. It may be necessary to alter the sequence of certain arguments or parts of the essay. Once happy with the content of the work, students should go through the essay systematically looking for grammatical errors, checking, say, word order, adjective endings, verbs and cases. If students read without any particular linguistic feature in mind it is very easy to overlook errors. Particular attention ought to be paid to the use of capital letters for the first letter of nouns and to the spelling of proper nouns.

Fostering a life-long love of literature

To conclude, today's students have a range of literary options and a variety of methodological approaches which they may adopt. If they have a clear idea of how they are approaching a text, they will be able to produce coherent essays based on first-hand knowledge of the text, but it is important to remember that students do not just study literature in order to pass an exam, but as part of the wider process of learning. One of the goals in teaching literature should be to foster a love of literature in its widest sense which will be life-long and will contribute to the students' general education and understanding of humanity.

References

1 It is an unfortunate fact in the 1990s that many university students may complete a degree without ever having read a whole book, be it fiction or non-fiction.

2 I refer throughout to the NEAB, which has two papers at GCSE, Basic and Higher, but other Exam Boards have a similar system of differentiation, although the names and number of levels may differ.

3 A reading programme is desirable at GCSE level, as outlined by Ann Swarbrick in her article 'Developing reading in Bushfield School' in *Autonomy in language learning,* London (CILT, 1990), pp. 89-92. Even where a school has a good reading programme, it is often the case that new 'A' level entrants from other schools or colleges will not all have had the same experience, and so it is necessary to devise an 'A' level reading programme sufficiently flexible to cope with the more and the less experienced reader.

4 Böseke H. and Wagner B., *Sind es noch die alten Farben? Nach Tschernobyl: Jugendliche und Erwachsene schreiben,* Weinheim (Beltz, 1987).

5 Ney N., *Sie haben mich zu einem Ausländer gemacht . . . ich bin einer geworden: Ausländer schreiben vom Leben bei uns,* Reinbek bei Hamburg (Rowohlt, 1984).

6 Ayse und Devrim, *Wo gehören wir hin?: Zwei türkische Mädchen erzählen,* Bornheim (Lamuv, 1983).

7 Although originally written in English, the autobiography deals with the life a German Jew and her deportation to Auschwitz, and is thus highly relevant to 'A' level German students. The account is written for the under tens and the language is particularly accessible.

8 The *Institut für Jugendbuchforschung* at the University of Frankfurt is one of the most important research centres both nationally and internationally.

9   In the majority of articles in *German Teaching* from 1993-95 on teaching specific literary texts there is no explicit mention of the justification for the critical approach adopted.

10 Selden R. and Widdowson P., *A Reader's Guide to Contemporary Literary Theory*, New York (Harvester Wheatsheaf, 1993), p.3.

Chapter 8

High attainers

Hilary MacDougall

In this chapter I shall be presenting and discussing the ways in which my colleagues and I at St Paul's Girls School, London, have sought to enhance the understanding, knowledge and achievements of able pupils in French and German over the last six years, using, in particular, an extended literature course.

Rationale

For some time prior to introducing this course, we had felt that the study of discrete texts in isolation, a very traditionalist approach to literature at 'A' level, offered a programme with grave shortcomings for motivated students whose interest in the history, geography and cultural attitudes of the foreign language was highly developed. At the same time, we remained committed to teaching literature, since our experience had shown that such pupils do in fact relish the opportunity to extend themselves beyond their immediate existence into more adult, and very different ways of dealing with and perceiving the world. Literature is an ideal medium for meeting that need, and for training students to empathise (not necessarily sympathise) with other lifestyles and value systems. Particularly problematic in this regard was the seventeenth century in France, where exposure to one comedy or one tragedy with no other acclimatisation, was often baffling or frustrating for the keen student, who very quickly realised the barriers set up by her own lack of knowledge of the period. Similar, and weighty, difficulties arose with the very definition of what literature written in German means, raising as it does questions of national and cultural identity in central Europe and demanding understanding of how the balance of power and historical perceptions are not fixed, but fluid. The bearing this has on contemporary politics is obvious. Last but not least, we feel that it is essential to continue to offer students access to the key element in a society's image of itself that its literature represents.

The diminution of the number of texts required by the board we follow (Oxford and Cambridge) from four to three gave us the chance to address these needs. Subsequently, this has become even more important in helping pupils familiarise themselves with literary terminology in the target language and giving them confidence in their ability to express themselves before embarking on a more detailed study of their set texts. In short, we believe that the course dovetails well with the linguistic and cultural content of current 'A' levels, and will do so even more with the arrival of modularity in 1997/98.

Structure

In setting up the course, we have sought to give as wide a range as possible within the limitations of the two terms it lasts (first two of lower sixth form). The formula which has emerged is: two twentieth century texts in the first term; excerpts from seventeenth century works together with a compulsory lecture to the whole year on the religious and political background to the seventeenth century in the second; and a (roughly) chronological set of selected poems throughout. The combination of texts varies from year to year, partly in accordance with what set texts they may go on to study, and we are always seeking to improve where we can. Below is a list of the texts we have used over the last six years in French.

List of texts used in the introduction to French literature course
St Paul's Girls' School 1989–1995

Prose works

(in full)

Balzac	*Le chef d'oeuvre inconnu*
	La messe de l'athée
	Facino Cane
Camus	*L'étranger*
	L'exil et le royaume (L'hôte, Les muets, La femme adultère only)
Duras	*Moderato cantabile*
Sartre	*Les jeux sont faits*

(extracts in translation)

Descartes	*Discours de la méthode* (childhood and education; the human mind; of God; that he exists; of the real distinction between the mind and the body)

Plays

(in full)

Ionesco	*Le roi se meurt*

(extracts)

Corneille	*Le Cid* (Act I, sc iii: pre-duel argument between Don Rodrigue and Don Diegue)
Racine	*Phèdre* (Act II, sc iv: revelation of Phèdre's love for Hyppolite) + *Phaedra britannica,* tr. Tony Harrison

---

Molière	*Le bourgeois gentilhomme* (Act II, sc4: *maître de philosophie* and M. Jourdain) *Tartuffe* (Act III, sc iii: Elmire and Tartuffe) + translations by Ranjit Bolt and Richard Wilbur

Poems

Villon	*Ballade des dames du temps jadis*
Ronsard	*Quand vous serez bien vieille* + W B Yeats: *When you are old and grey*
Baudelaire	*La chevelure, Correspondances*
Rimbaud	*Le dormeur du val* + Rupert Brooke: *The soldier* and Wilfred Owen: *Futility*
Verlaine	*Sonnet boiteux*
Apollinaire	*Les femmes, Le pont Mirabeau*
Eluard	*Critique de la poésie*
Desnos	*La peste*
Follain	*Les siècles, La pomme rouge*
Jaccottet	*Dans un tourbillon de neige*
Reda	*Le bracelet perdu*

Case history: poetry

The use of poetry has been one area of particular discovery, viz. how accessible in fact our students have found it and how richly they benefit from very short pieces of text. Initially, many pupils do express apprehension, although most have studied some poetry for GCSE, this tends to be confined to very contemporaneous material, often chosen to mirror their own experience, and they are rarely familiar with questions of form or rhetoric. In approaching the poetry of another language, such questions have of necessity to be dealt with, since there cannot be proper comprehension of the text without them. So students actually learn more, paradoxically, as a result of the obvious barriers of language.

To help them as they start, I issue a check list for them to use until they are more accustomed to poetic analysis. (All materials, other than the originals, are created by the department; the examples given here are my own.)

Poetry appreciation: notes for hesitant beginners

Like all study, the art of literary and poetry appreciation is largely a question of practice. To some extent, it is a technique which can be learnt, though clearly there are and always will be differences in the subtlety and finesse of readers' interpretations. Below are some key points which you must **always** bear in mind when reading a poem and indeed frequently also with prose.

A **Form: what effect it produces.** Don't just describe what the form of a particular poem is and leave it at that. If you can't think how it is significant, then don't mention it. You should familiarise yourself gradually with some of the commoner poetic forms.

B **Use of language.** Ask yourself what **kind** of language is being used. Is it lyric, straightforward, obscure, allusive, repetitive, direct, ambiguous, ironic, melancholic, descriptive, emotive, clichéd? It won't be all of these things at once, but it is almost certain to be more than just one of them. Don't be too easily satisfied by your own analysis. Check several times to make sure you have thought of everything.

C **Do not 'jump in'** and start to impute things to the poem that aren't actually there. This is a very common fault, stemming from one's own assumptions about how a subject should be treated, or even the stereotypes that exist in your own mind.

D **Mood:** this really should emerge from your discussion of use of language. This is what language is doing: creating an effect and impact. It is up to you to decide what these effects and impacts are.

E **Be alert to allusions and associations of language.** For a proper appreciation of European literatures, this in particular means that you must be well versed in Greco-Roman mythology, the Old and New Testaments, fables and fairy stories, and to a lesser extent, Anglo-Saxon and Celtic mythology. If this sounds daunting, you're right, but also remember that being familiar with these will infinitely enhance your capacity to understand music, painting, architecture, even references in the newspapers and ordinary speech. Literature cannnot be studied in isolation from life, since it is a reflection of it.

F More difficult to do is **to be aware of historical references.** These will not always be relevant, but usually the subject matter of a piece will direct you towards its topicality by its very nature, e.g. a political or social poem is unlikely to have been written in a vacuum.

G **Ambiguity:** remember how language conceals and/or merely hints. Ever listened to a politician talking? You must constantly be on the alert to pinpoint and interpret these half-utterances.

H Closely related to ambiguity is **irony.** One of the most difficult concepts to come to grips with. Remember that apart from concealing and hinting language can also appear to be saying the opposite, or at least not quite the same as, what it means. Don't take the words at their face value. Language's persuasiveness may often depend on its ability to deceive, to mock, to show things suddenly in a different light. All these things may be effected through the use of irony.

I Lastly, **don't panic** or think *this is too difficult for me.* Practice is the best way to improve. Remember that your own powers of self-expression can only get better by understanding how other people manipulate language

This checklist is designed to make the process as painless as possible, and to stress that appreciation can be within the reach of those pupils who believe that they are not particularly gifted in this field. As with all learning, enabling and encouraging is half the battle, and it is heartening to discover how students take to poetry if they are not given pre-emptive remarks like *this is going to be very difficult* or even denied access at all: *we're not going to do this because it's beyond you.*

It is true that, when students read E, there are usually expressions of disbelief (*you don't really mean all of these, do you?*), but I use this to gauge how much input a particular class needs in this area. Research can then be targeted, with the added advantage that this encourages independent learning and teaches them study skills; they can then be asked to carry out project work in an area they have discovered and present this in the target language to fellow students. One class has in the past selected favourite or key passages from the Old and New Testament, which led to more intensive study of the parables, many of which were completely new to pupils. In a recent case, a pupil prepared a presentation on Poussin as a result of her study of the seventeenth century, when issues of neo-classical aesthetics and subject matter had begun to interest her. So this kind of research really can be used to improve the quality of their cultural understanding and of their confidence in the language, whilst retaining considerable flexibility with regard to individual pupils' interests. They are invariably appreciative of it at the end.

Below is an example of what pupils receive. The biographical information may be in either English or the target language, depending on the pupils' level. (See Appendix 1 for an example of the use of the target language for the same purpose.)

Sonnet boiteux

Ah! vraiment c'est triste, ah! vraiment ça finit trop mal.

Il n'est pas permis d'être à ce point infortuné.

Ah! vraiment c'est trop la mort du naïf animal

Qui voit tout son sang couler sous son regard fané.

Londres fume et crie. O quelle ville de la Bible!

Le gaz flambe et nage et les enseignes sont vermeilles.

Et les maisons dans leur ratatinement terrible

Epouvantent comme un sénat de petites vieilles.

Tout l'affreux passé saute, piaule, miaule et glapit

Dans le brouillard rose et jaune et sale des sohos

Avec des indeeds et des all rights et des haos.

Non vraiment c'est trop un martyre sans espérance.

Non vraiment cela finit trop mal, vraiment c'est triste:

O le feu du ciel sur cette ville de la Bible!

Paul Verlaine (1844–1896)

Born in Metz near the German border, Verlaine early showed a fluency with traditional forms, but was soon to explore a poetic world more remarkable for the evocative nature of its images and the haunting irregularity of its lines. Much of his *Fêtes galantes* has been likened to the painting of the early eighteenth century artist, Watteau, in the way figures, dressed for some unspecified masque, move in and out of a neo-classical gardenscape in pursuit of Eros, but pursued by time. Verlaine's meeting with the younger poet, Rimbaud, brought emotional crisis (his marriage never recovered) but poetic innovation. He experimented more and more boldly with irregular forms and increasingly used them to bring out the sense of transience and conflict which characterise his best later poetry. Verlaine spent two years in prison (1873–5) on conviction of having inflicted grievous bodily harm to Rimbaud in a drunken argument (Verlaine shot at him twice, slightly wounding Rimbaud); during this time, he endeavoured to be reconciled with his wife and the Catholic church, and for some time after his release his writing reflected his devotional interests. His later years were marked, however, by a decline into the alcoholism and debauch he had shown in youth, although, ironically, his reputation as a master of poetic line was being established at the same time amongst a generation of younger writers such as Mallarmé.

Notes:

You will find Gustave Doré's engravings of nineteenth century London a useful and illuminating complement to this poem; as, on a more general level, a comparison with Dickens' vision of London.

Why do you think the poem has the title it does? Look carefully at the form and metre: how do they relate to the content of the poem?

What sort of image of London do you gain from the poem? Why is London *une ville de la Bible*?

Verlaine wrote this poem out of his experience of several years' teaching in England (Sussex and Lincolnshire) after his release from prison: how does he use London to reflect upon himself and his past?

What strikes you about the use of language? What registers are to be found here? What is the effect of introducing English into the poem?

Sonnet boiteux has proved to be a particularly rewarding text because of the density of cultural and linguistic information and reference (we have found Apollinaire's *Les femmes* and Desnos' *La peste* to be other especially successful poems in this sense, always provoking new and unexpected responses from students). A fruitful point of entry into practically any poem we choose is to stress the nature of the imagery and the actual mental picture created in the reader's (i.e. the student's) mind. Getting them to compare what they are 'seeing' can frequently produce both illuminating and hilarious results. It is also excellent for pointing out errors or carelessness in their straightforward reading of the text, i.e. where a pupil 'sees' something for which there is no justification in the words used, or for deciding where it is valid to invoke associations.

In this particular poem, **particularly** evocative are the images of London recreated. This can provoke discussion of what distinguishes nineteenth century London from its late twentieth century counterpart, what an industrial revolution means and how it changes society. Pupils have in the past researched and brought in photos which illustrate historically what Verlaine is using poetically. Many pupils are unfamiliar with the London smog and what caused it; again, this has a practical bearing on discussion elsewhere of issues such as environmental pollution. The use of onomatopeia is well developed, and students do enjoy the effects this creates (even the most sophisticated are happy to try the sound effects out — the element of discovery in just rolling the language around the tongue should not be underestimated. (*Ratatinement* is a favourite.) *La ville de la Bible*, evoking the cities of the plain, demonstrates to pupils the importance of picking up allusions, and how subtly these can be echoed to underline the universality of experience across time (e.g. *les enseignes sont vermeilles* reminds how red is associated with prostitution). Perhaps the most gratifying aspect of teaching this poem is students' gradual realisation of how form underlies content: the actual smog of nineteenth century London, and the confusion it creates, becomes a metaphor for the confusion of the mind in the poem, while the uneven number of syllables makes the poem, from a prosodic point of view, quite literally lame — and this comes full circle to allude to the sulphurous presence of Mephistopheles himself.

Extracts from seventeenth century texts

The examples given are deliverately chosen to expose the students to a gamut of differing preoccupations which they might otherwise find alien. The extract from *Le Cid* can be used both to make pupils reflect on what they understand by honour and also to question those assumptions: typically, they tend to regard honour as a question of personal conscience only, and fail to see a social perspective; in situations such as these the cosmopolitan nature of our classes is especially beneficial, enabling us as it does to make contemporary cross-cultural comparisons. This scene is also excellent for teaching students painlessly about the alexandrine, since a significant proportion of the hostility of the two men is underlined by Corneille's use of 'hostile' hemistichs — and, perhaps contrary to expectations, able pupils are intrigued by the notion of formal prosody. This can lead into lengthy and detailed discussion of other forms and, again, to pupils' own research for examples of poems that they themselves present to the rest of the group. In certain circumstances, comparison of treatment of a theme across different languages can be enlightening; thus, I will always look at Rupert Brook's *The soldier* and Wilfred Owen's *Futility* (see Appendix 2) in conjunction with Rimbaud's *Le dormeur du val.* This can be easily adapted to suit the tastes and needs of individual groups and teachers alike.

It is fortunate, in the case of some seventeenth century theatre, that good translations by reputable authors in their own right exist. The use of comparative translation is another method of introducing pupils to questions of register, translation or traduction of the original, and idiom. Pupils are asked to read two translations of *Tartuffe* (in this case, by Bolt and Wilbur) and comment on which they prefer, and why. They are often surprised by how tricky this is, and it almost always leads to discussion of some very tiny pieces of the text, something which again provides good training in the careful attention to detail which, as I am constantly pointing out to them, is not just a literary requirement, but a requirement in communication in all walks of life. Many comic topics are present in this scene and in that from *Le bourgeois gentilhomme,* and pupils are invariably inventive in their choice of examples to illustrate these from their television or film watching. And they are, to paraphrase M. Jourdan himself, always delighted to discover that *I've been watching comic topoi (?) all my life, and never even knew it?!*

Since we found that following such a course as I have outlined above produced noticeable improvements in students' ability to tackle a full or longer text, and considerable personal satisfaction in terms of what they felt they had gained culturally, we have now introduced it into our German programme. Here there has been a greater need to provide pupils with 'ready-made' lists of critical vocabulary and expressions which they are then encouraged to appropriate, rather than finding them out as necessity dictates. Here is an example of such material.

Kritischer Wortschatz

darstellen, zeigen, verfassen, der Verfasser, wählen, schildern, beschreiben

sich um etwas handeln, handeln von, sich abspielen

die Geschichte, die Erzählung, die Novelle, der Roman, der Aufsatz

das Thema, die Hauptsache, der Stoff, die Lösung, der Ausgangspunkt

wirken auf, eine Wirkung haben, wirkungsvoll, eindrucksvoll, kräftig

der Sinn, die Einbildung, die Einbildungskraft, die Vorstellung, sich (dat) etwas vorstellen

der Raum, die innerliche/innere Welt, die äußere Welt, der Hintergrund, der Vordergrund, in den Vordergrund rücken/stellen

das Interesse an . . ., das Interesse des Schriftstellers gilt der Situation der Frauen am Ende des neunzehnten Jahrhunderts . . .

lebhaft, lebenstreu, realistisch, phantasievoll, unheimlich, ausführlich, rätselhaft, geheimnisvoll, gruselig, symbolisch, märchenhaft, unwahrscheinlich

er schildert die dunklen Triebe der Menschen in all ihrer Grausamkeit

der Stil: lebendig, trocken, gewandt, flüssig, bilderreich

einen Widerspruch erklären, im Widerspruch zu, der innere Widerspruch, rechtfertigen

die Meinung, die Absicht, beabsichtigen, die Ansicht, eine Ansicht vertreten, das Ziel

bedeuten, bedeutungsvoll, auf etwas hinweisen, auf etwas aufmerksam machen, zu verstehen geben, beeinflussen

er weiß, die ländliche Lebensweise genau zu beschreiben . . .

die Idee, die Ideologie, der Glaube an, die Glaubwürdigkeit

If such material is built around an author or text, able students soon begin to use it as their own, and develop their own critical lexicon. As with the French course, there has been no prescription about what pupils will or will not find difficult; a recent class studied *Urfaust* in the period corresponding to the seventeenth century introduction in French, and this text proved especially successful, confounding more conventional notions about what can be managed. Although this was a group with one or two highly literary pupils, by no means all were — yet the debates unleashed in literary discussion generated great passions and enthusiasms in all the class. Interestingly, the high incidence and greater acceptability of single parenthood in late twentieth century British society appeared not to dilute strong feelings about the nature of human relationships, and the good and evil associated therewith, at all; no-one felt Gretchen's plight to be anachronistic or irrelevant, whilst discussion of the role of Mephistopheles prompted quite sophisticated investigation concerning the extent to which evil can be said to be external or internal.

Lastly, at the end of the two-year course, we issue a questionnaire to students to find out what has motivated them, and what they have liked and disliked as a way of ensuring that we continue to deliver a course of study which is of high quality and which stretches them sufficiently.

Over the last six years, therefore, we have been able to evolve a literature programme which is both testing and rewarding for pupils and teachers alike. This study has overlapped with all the topics they cover in the study of the living language, helps to enhance their confidence and range orally in the target language, makes them alert to questions of rhetoric and provides them with at least the beginnings of an understanding of Europe's cultural heritage, as well as of the more negative aspects of its imperial legacy. It has certainly vindicated a belief that today's students do have the capacity, and the enthusiasm, to approach literature and that they benefit in multifarious ways from it.

Appendix 1

Theodor Storm

In 1817 als erstes Kind des Advokaten Johann Storm in Husum (Schleswig-Holstein) geboren. Von 1837 bis 1842 studierte er Jura an den Kieler und Berliner Universitäten, zu dieser Zeit begann er, seine ersten Gedichte zu schreiben. In 1843 kehrte er als Advokat nach Husum zurück, wo er drei Jahre später Ehe mit Constanze Esmarch schloss. In 1849 wurde er durch seine Novelle *Immensee* international bekannt, aber in 1852 wurde er der Kassierung seiner Advokatenanstellung wegen gezwungen, sich in Berlin niederzulassen. Hier wurde er Mitglied eines Literarkreises, und schloss mit Theodor Fontane, dem Schriftsteller, Freundschaft. Aber kurz nach der Rückkehr nach Husum starb seine Frau an Kindbettfieber; er was also imstande, ein Jahr später sich mit seiner Geliebten von vielen Jahren, Dorothea Jensen, zu verheiraten. Trotz seiner Berufstätigkeit dichtete er während dieser Jahre ununterbrochen. In 1880 tritt er ins Privatleben zurück; kurz vor seinem Tod an Magenkrebs vollendete er die Novelle *Der Schimmelreiter,* die gewöhnlicherweise als der Gipfel seines dichterischen Lebens gilt.

Appendix 2

The soldier

If I should die, think only this of me,
That there's some corner of a foreign field
That is forever England. There shall be
In that rich earth a richer dust concealed,
A dust whom England bore, shaped, made aware,
Gave, once, her flowers to love, her ways to roam,
A body of England's, breathing English air,
Washed by the rivers, blest by suns of home.
And think, this heart, all evil shed away,
A pulse in the Eternal mind, no less
Gives somewhere back the thoughts by England given,
Her sights and sounds; dreams happy as her day,
And laughter, learnt of friends; and gentleness,
In hearts at peace, under an English heaven.

Rupert Brooke (1887–1915)

Futility

Move him into the sun —
Gently its touch awoke him once,
At home, whispering of fields unsown.
Always it woke him, even in France,
Until this morning and this snow.
If anything might rouse him now
The kind old sun will know.
Think how it wakes the seeds —

Woke, once, the clays of a cold star.
Are limbs, so dear-achieved, are sides,
Full-nerved — still warm — too hard to stir?
Was it for this the clay grew tall?
— O what made fatuous sunbeams toil
To break earth's sleep at all?

Wilfred Owen (1893–1918)

Epilogue

The transition to higher education

Gareth Thomas

There has been a large increase in the number of students who study a foreign language in higher education on a 'modern languages' degree course, as part of a joint degree, in a variety of combinations (many of them vocational), or as a subsidiary subject or module. Indeed it is becoming increasingly difficult to provide enough resources to cope with the demand, especially at *ab initio* level.

But how do more advanced students who have studied a language to 'A' level cope with the transition to higher education? Does a good grade at 'A' level properly prepare them for further study of their chosen language?

It is evident that students in many disciplines other than modern languages perceive a need to be able to communicate with the rest of the world using the target language in their future lives.

So what qualities do successful foreign language learners in higher education display? The following suggestions are based on my own observations in the classroom:

Independence: they do not require constant injections of support or aid in order to carry out their learning goals.

Motivation: they have a high motivation to communicate and are usually active investigators into the nature of the language they are learning and its societal context.

Interaction: they interact freely and supportively with others, developing communicative strategies as they do so (linguistic, paralinguistic).

Cultural openness: they are open-minded and open-hearted with regard to other cultures and individuals. This attitude will open doors for them and create opportunities for further linguistic progress. They enjoy being 'cultural mediators' in meetings with people from different language communities.

Language aptitude: they have a good 'feel' for intonation/mood, inductive language learning ability, etc.

Teachers of foreign languages need, therefore, to encourage in their students not only an open and tolerant attitude to the target language country and its culture but also a spirit of enterprise.

Students need to be able to work independently — very often in open access language centres using educational technology. This requires self motivation and a high degree of self discipline. They also have to use the language they learn to interact with others, to manipulate it whilst being aware of the skills involved in communicating. Added to this is the need to combine an intellectual inquisitiveness with a genuine feel for the language, which requires continual use and practice. If students have not at least begun to acquire these skills in the sixth form then their task in higher education will be that much harder.

Successful students of foreign languages have learned how to learn a language and accept that they have to put on a number of different 'hats' as they do so:

- **actor:** willing to take risks, even appear foolish.
- **guesser:** looks for clues in context.
- **experimenter:** tries out newly acquired knowledge.
- **communicator:** uses paraphrases borrowed from L1, circumlocutes, checks hearer understanding.
- **organiser:** looks for patterns in the language.
- **absorber:** looks for social rules, cultural taboos, intonation, gesture, etc.

The emerging sixth form student needs to have enough self confidence not to worry about making mistakes, be flexible in the manipulation of the language, be on the lookout for **new** language and be aware of the cultural and social elements so closely connected with communication. Such students will have been taught in the sixth form to enjoy the challenge of pushing themselves as far as they can and will have found that experience enjoyable.

Successful foreign language students in higher education seek exposure to the foreign language and its culture. They seek out every opportunity to come into contact with the real thing, e.g. cinema, clubs, TV, newspapers, magazines, bar room conversation, etc in order to get a variety of different social contexts. Of course it is easy for students who have the opportunity to study or work in the target language country to do these things. But even without this direct experience of the country, those who have had the opportunity to meet authentic materials in the classroom and been encouraged to try on the different 'hats' mentioned above, will approach their language learning in the right spirit.

A degree of autonomy, a willingness to use the target language, the self-confidence to experiment, familiarity with authentic materials, enthusiasm for the language and its culture, all these qualities from the 'A' level course will help make the transition from sixth form to higher education successful.